THE

SAN

T H E   B O O K   O F

SANDWICHES

LOUISE STEELE

Photography by
PAUL GRATER

HPBooks
a division of
PRICE STERN SLOAN
Los Angeles

ANOTHER BEST SELLING VOLUME FROM HPBOOKS

HPBooks
A division of Price Stern Sloan, Inc.
11150 Olympic Boulevard
Los Angeles, California 90064

9 8 7 6 5 4 3

By arrangement with Salamander Books Ltd. and Merehurst Press, London.

This book was created by Merehurst Limited.
Ferry House, 51-57 Lacy Road, Putney, London SW15

Commissioned and directed by Merehurst Limited
Designer: Roger Daniels
Home Economist: Stephen Wheeler
Photographer: Paul Grater
Color separation by Kentscan Limited
Printed in Belgium by Proost International Book Production

Library of Congress Cataloging-in-Publication Data

Steele, Louise.
     The book of sandwiches.

     Includes Index.
     1. Sandwiches   I. Title.
TX818.R26   1988   641.8'4—dc19   88-21323
ISBN0-89586-789-3 (pbk.)

CONTENTS

INTRODUCTION

The sandwich idea has certainly come a long way since the original notion was created by John Montague, fourth Earl of Sandwich. This gentleman—so the story goes—being such a keen gambler, did not want to leave his cards to eat. So he asked that his cold beef be placed between two slices of bread, thus making it easy to eat and at the same time allowing him to carry on with the game!

Even today the sandwich we enjoy is often similar to the original—two slices of bread enclosing a filling. The variations, however, on this theme are almost endless, as *The Book of Sandwiches* shows with over 100 beautifully illustrated recipes. There is surely a sandwich here to suit all tastes and almost any occasion—pleasing the eye as well as the palate. Sandwiches are a great way to make the most of the marvelous selection of breads now available—whole-wheat, light or dark rye, pumpernickel, French, pitta, bagels and so on. Delicious and imaginative fillings and toppings make them memorable.

These recipes include open-face sandwiches, popular in Scandinavia and Germany, where only a single slice of bread is used and the topping decoratively arranged. Layered sandwiches with a variety of lavish fillings, tea sandwich ideas, dainty pinwheels where the filling is rolled up in the bread and then cut in slices and stuffed sandwiches using hollowed out loaves or rolls will make you want to experiment with new kinds of sandwiches. All kinds of creative ideas for grilled and toasted snacks to baked and deep-fried sandwiches are also included.

You will find interesting international recipes such as Pan Bagna, page 63, New Orleans Oyster Loaf, page 64, and Croque Monsieur, page 74, from France. Directions are given for preparing luscious sweet sandwiches as well as more elegant party ideas in a tempting assortment of attractive bite-size nibbles and decorative canapés.

Whether you are filling a lunchbox, packing a picnic, planning a party or simply wanting something deliciously hot and tasty for supper, there is no doubt you will find a tempting sandwich idea here to suit the occasion.

INGREDIENTS

We are almost spoiled with the wonderful selection of breads now available from bakeries, supermarkets and health food stores. Make the most of them—and what better way than in sandwiches!

Crusty or soft, sliced or unsliced, breads come in an amazing variety of shapes, sizes and types. There are floury-topped or rich glazed loaves and rolls sprinkled with seeds or cracked wheat, nutritious nutty-flavored wholewheat, loaves and multi-grain breads, plus those enriched with added wheat germ or bran. Rye breads (popular in Scandinavia and central Europe) range from light ryes and caraway-seeded types to black pumpernickel bread, favored in Germany. Popular French bread loaves, available in whole-wheat, are sometimes seeded.

Look for the more unusual breads in Continental, Jewish and ethnic foodshops: Greek sesame bread (daktyla); Indian nan bread; rich plaited Jewish egg bread (challah); bagels—to name but a few. Try the unfamiliar types—you may discover a new favorite. Some loaves and rolls may not always be the ideal shape for making sandwiches and rolls, but remember a sandwich need not be conventional in appearance to be exceptionally good to eat! Choose the bread to suit the style of sandwich—nice and crusty for thicker types; firm-textured rye or pumpernickel for open-face sandwiches and so on. As sandwiches are a matter of personal preference, the breads recommended in many recipes are a guide, leaving the final decision to you. In other recipes, such as pinwheel sandwiches where lengthwise slices from an uncut loaf are needed, it is wise to use the bread suggested to ensure good results.

Crusts on or off? It's up to you unless the recipe states otherwise. But the thicker the sandwich, the more reason to leave crusts on.

Always use softened butter right up to the edges of each slice to avoid tearing the bread and to prevent moistness from fillings from seeping into the bread and making it soggy. When more than two slices of bread are used (in a layered sandwich for example),

the center slices need buttering on both sides; this is stated in the recipes.

For economy and when using a well flavored filling, a soft margarine instead of butter (or a mixture of the two) may be used. Flavored butters are quick and easy to make and help make the sandwich tasty, especially if it is a simple affair. Select a flavor to complement the filling, such as mustard or horseradish butter with beef or ham, lemon juice and a pinch of cayenne pepper with smoked salmon or herb or curry butter with egg, cheese and chicken. Beat the flavoring into softened butter or margarine and spread it over the bread slices before adding fillings. Quick ideas include a little anchovy or curry paste, crushed garlic, chopped fresh chives or parsley (or any herb of your choice—basil with a tomato filling is excellent), mustard, tomato paste, a few drops of hot-pepper sauce or lemon juice.

Remember too, savory butters make a pretty garnish for open-face sandwiches .and party canapés. Either spoon mixture into a pastry bag fitted with a star tube and pipe as required, or spread the butter mixture onto foil, chill until firm and cut with aspic cutters.

Fortunately the requirements for making sandwiches are few. Of course good bread and deliciously generous fillings are essential, but little special equipment is needed. A good bread knife is important for slicing evenly and cutting in serving portions. Sandwich makers, although useful, are not essential for making toasted or fried sandwiches. Don't despair if you haven't got one—a skillet does the job just as well.

You will find, however, a selection of cutters, pastry bags and tubes and tiny aspic cutters are worth investing in for adding special flair to the decorative sandwiches and party canapés. Other useful additions to help widen your repertoire include small boat-shaped tartlet pans for Ham & Cheese Boats, page 109, small round pans for Vegetable Curry Pies, page 77, and individual fluted pans for Sweety Pies, page 90.

Cucumber-Mint Coolers

1/4 cucumber, peeled, thinly sliced
1/2 teaspoon salt
2 teaspoons finely chopped fresh mint
1/8 teaspoon sugar
1/4 teaspoon fresh lemon juice
3 tablespoons butter, softened
4 thin slices whole-wheat or white bread,
    crusts removed
Pepper to taste
Sprigs of fresh mint to garnish

Place cucumber slices in a sieve. Sprinkle with salt; press down with a saucer. Let drain 30 minutes. Pat cucumber slices dry on paper towels. In a small bowl, mix finely chopped mint, sugar, lemon juice and butter until soft and creamy. Butter bread. Arrange cucumber slices on 2 slices of buttered bread. Season with pepper. Cover with remaining slices of buttered bread. Press together firmly. Cut in squares or fingers. Garnish with mint. Makes 8 pieces.

Salmon Pinwheels

2 (1/4-inch-thick) lengthwise slices white
   uncut sandwich bread,
   crusts removed
1/3 cup butter, softened
3 tablespoons finely chopped fresh
   parsley
1 teaspoon fresh lemon juice
1/8 teaspoon cayenne pepper
4 ozs. thinly sliced smoked salmon
Pepper to taste
Lemon twists and sprigs of fresh parsley
   to garnish

Using a rolling pin, roll each slice of
bread firmly to flatten. In a small bowl,
combine butter, 1 tablespoon of
chopped parsley, lemon juice and
cayenne pepper. Spread 2/3 of butter
mixture on flattened bread. Arrange
slices of salmon on buttered bread and
season with pepper. Roll up each slice,
jelly-roll style, starting from a short
side. Spread remaining butter on outside of rolls and coat evenly in remaining chopped parsley. Wrap rolls tightly
in plastic wrap. Chill at least 2 hours.
Remove plastic wrap. Cut each roll in 7
slices. Garnish with lemon twists and
parsley sprigs. Makes 14 pieces.

Variation: Coat 1 buttered roll with
chopped parsley and the other roll in
paprika. Chill and cut in slices.

Lobster Rounds

6 ozs. cooked fresh or frozen lobster,
  thawed if frozen, chopped
2 small stalks celery, finely chopped
3 tablespoons mayonnaise
1/8 teaspoon cayenne pepper
Salt to taste
1/4 cup butter, softened
1 teaspoon fresh lemon juice
1 tablespoon chopped fresh parsley
6 slices pumpernickel bread
8 thin slices cucumber
8 radishes and 8 sprigs of fresh parsley
  to garnish

In a medium-size bowl, combine lobster, celery, 2 tablespoons of mayonnaise and cayenne pepper. Season with salt. Mix well. In a small bowl, mix butter, lemon juice and chopped parsley. Using a round 2-inch fluted or plain cutter, cut 4 rounds from each slice of bread. Butter 8 bread rounds on 1 side and remaining 16 on both sides. Cover 8 rounds buttered on 1 side with 1 cucumber slice each. Spread with 1/2 of lobster mixture. Top with 8 bread rounds buttered on both sides. Press together lightly. Spread with remaining lobster mixture and top with remaining bread rounds buttered on both sides. Spread tops of buttered bread rounds with remaining mayonnaise. Cut radishes in small wedge-shaped slices. Arrange in spoke-like fashion on top of each bread round. Garnish with radishes and sprigs of parsley. Makes 8 pieces.

Variation: Substitute white crabmeat or chopped shrimp for lobster.

Brie & Apple Slices on Rye

3 tablespoons butter, softened
2 tablespoons chopped walnuts
4 square slices light rye bread, crusts
    removed
4 (1/4-inch-thick) lengthwise slices Brie
    cheese
1/2 Green Delicious apple
1/2 Red Delicious apple
1 tablespoon fresh lemon juice
Sprigs of fresh watercress to garnish

In a small bowl, combine butter and walnuts. Butter bread. Cut slices of cheese in half crosswise. Arrange 2 pieces of cheese on each slice of buttered bread. Cut apples in quarters and remove cores; do not peel. Thinly slice apples and brush with lemon juice. Arrange overlapping alternate slices of green and red apples over cheese. Cut each tea sandwich diagonally in half. Garnish with watercress. Makes 8 pieces.

Spicy Shrimp Tempters

4 ozs. peeled cooked fresh or frozen
   shrimp, thawed if frozen, drained,
   coarsely chopped
2 tablespoons Thousand Island dressing
2 teaspoons tomato paste
1 teaspoon prepared creamed
   horseradish
Salt and pepper to taste
3 tablespoons butter, softened
4 square slices light rye bread, crusts
   removed
Sprigs of fresh watercress
4 small radicchio leaves
8 peeled cooked small shrimp

In a medium-size bowl, combine shrimp, dressing, tomato paste and horseradish. Season with salt and pepper. Mix well. Butter bread. Reserve 2 sprigs of watercress. Cover 2 slices of buttered bread with remaining watercress and top with shrimp mixture. Cover with radicchio leaves. Place remaining slices of buttered bread on top. Press together firmly. Cut diagonally in quarters. Secure a small shrimp to each triangle with a wooden pick. Garnish with reserved watercress. Makes 8 pieces.

Variations: Substitute thinly sliced sesame seed Greek bread for light rye bread; do not remove crusts.

Substitute crisp green lettuce leaves for raddichio leaves.

Egg-Chive Tea Sandwiches

2 hard-cooked eggs, peeled
2 tablespoons mayonnaise
2 teaspoons chopped fresh chives
Salt and pepper to taste
1/4 cup butter, softened
2 large thin slices whole-wheat bread
2 large thin slices white bread
8 stuffed green olives and tiny sprigs of
    fresh chervil to garnish

In a medium-size bowl, mash eggs finely with a fork. Add mayonnaise and chives. Season with salt and pepper. Mix well. Butter bread. Using a 2-inch round cutter, cut 4 rounds from each slice of bread. Cover whole-wheat bread rounds with egg mixture. Using a 1/4-inch clover-leaf shaped cutter, cut shapes from center of white bread rounds; place on top of egg mixture. Press down lightly. Cut each olive in 3 thick slices. Garnish each tea sandwich with 3 olive slices and chervil. Makes 8 pieces.

Variation: Substitute watercress (green part only) for chives. Lightly flavor egg mixture with a small amount of curry paste.

Piquant Salmon Treats

6 ozs. salmon steak
1 teaspoon fresh lemon juice
Salt and pepper to taste
1 to 2 teaspoons capers, drained
3 tablespoons mayonnaise
3 cocktail gherkin pickles, chopped
1 green onion, chopped
2 (1/4-inch-thick) lengthwise slices uncut
    white sandwich bread, crusts removed
3 tablespoons butter, softened
Paprika
Sprigs of fresh parsley to garnish

Preheat oven to 350F (175C). Butter a sheet of foil large enough to enclose salmon. Place salmon on buttered foil. Sprinkle with lemon juice and season with salt and pepper. Wrap foil to enclose salmon. Place on a baking sheet. Bake in preheated oven 25 minutes. Cool, then skin and bone salmon. Flake salmon into a medium-size bowl. Dry capers on paper towels and chop finely. Add capers, mayonnaise, pickles and green onion to salmon. Season with salt and pepper. Mix well. Using a rolling pin, lightly roll bread to flatten slightly. Butter 1 slice on 1 side and remaining slice on both sides. Using 2-inch fluted round cutter, cut 8 rounds from bread buttered on 1 side. Cover bread rounds with salmon mixture, reserving a small amount. Using same cutter, cut 8 rounds from remaining bread buttered on both sides. Using a 3/4-inch fluted round cutter, cut centers from bread rounds and discard centers. Sprinkle bread rounds with paprika and place on salmon. Press together lightly. Spoon reserved salmon mixture into centers. Garnish with parsley. Makes 8 pieces.

Chicken-Relish Swirls

3 ozs. cold cooked skinned chicken
2 teaspoons mango chutney, chopped
2 teaspoons mayonnaise
3 tablespoons finely chopped green bell
   pepper
2 green onions, finely chopped
2 cocktail gherkin pickles, finely
   chopped
Salt and pepper to taste
3 medium-thick slices white bread, crusts
   removed
1/4 cup butter, softened
About 21 stuffed green olives
Sprigs of fresh Italian parsley to garnish

In a food processor fitted with the metal blade, process chicken to a puree or mince finely with a sharp knife. In a medium-size bowl, combine chicken puree, chutney, mayonnaise, bell pepper, green onions and pickles. Season with salt and pepper. Mix well. Using a rolling pin, firmly flatten each slice of bread. Butter bread, then spread with chicken mixture. Arrange a row of olives along 1 short edge of each slice. Roll up each piece, jelly-roll style. Wrap each roll tightly in plastic wrap. Chill at least 2 hours. Cut each roll at a slight diagonal angle in 7 slices. Garnish with parsley. Makes 21 pieces.

Variations: Substitute cocktail gherkin pickles for stuffed olives.

Substitute cold cooked turkey for chicken, or use a mixture of chicken and ham.

Deviled Crab Treats

4 ozs. fresh or frozen white crabmeat,
    thawed if frozen
2 tablespoons mayonnaise
Few drops fresh lemon juice
Few drops hot-pepper sauce
1/4 teaspoon dry mustard
Salt and pepper to taste
3 tablespoons butter, softened
4 thin slices whole-wheat or white bread,
    crusts removed
1 or 2 crisp lettuce leaves, finely
    shredded
1 teaspoon paprika
Lemon twist and sprigs of fresh
    watercress to garnish

Flake crabmeat into a medium-size bowl. Reserve 1 teaspoon of mayonnaise. Add remaining mayonnaise, lemon juice, hot-pepper sauce and dry mustard to crabmeat. Season with salt and pepper. Mix lightly. Butter bread. Spread 2 slices of buttered bread with crabmeat mixture. Top with shredded lettuce. Cover with remaining slices of buttered bread. Press together firmly. Cut diagonally in quarters. Very lightly spread reserved mayonnaise on every other edge of each sandwich. Dip mayonnaise coated edges into paprika. Garnish with lemon twist and watercress. Makes 8 pieces.

Variations: Substitute peeled, thinly sliced cucumber for shredded lettuce.

Coat edges in finely chopped chives instead of paprika, or coat half in paprika and remainder in chives.

Avocado Bites

1 tablespoon safflower oil
1 teaspoon fresh lemon juice
1/8 teaspoon sugar
1/8 teaspoon dry mustard
Salt and pepper to taste
1 small ripe avocado
1/4 cup butter, softened
2 large thin slices white bread, crusts
  removed
1 large thin slice whole-wheat bread,
  crusts removed
Radish flowers to garnish

To make dressing, in a small bowl, whisk safflower oil, lemon juice, sugar and dry mustard. Season with salt and pepper. Whisk until well combined. Cut avocado in half and remove pit. Peel avocado; cut in thin slices. Drizzle with dressing. Butter white bread on 1 side and whole-wheat bread on both sides. Arrange 1/2 of avocado slices over 1 slice of buttered white bread. Cover with buttered whole-wheat bread. Arrange remaining avocado slices over buttered whole-wheat bread. Top with remaining slices of buttered white bread. Press together firmly. Cut in quarters to form squares, then cut each square diagonally in half to form triangles. Garnish with radish flowers. Makes 8 pieces.

Variations: Add a slice of Westphalian ham, cut to fit bread, before adding avocado.

Cut sandwich in dainty shapes using heart and diamond-shaped cutters.

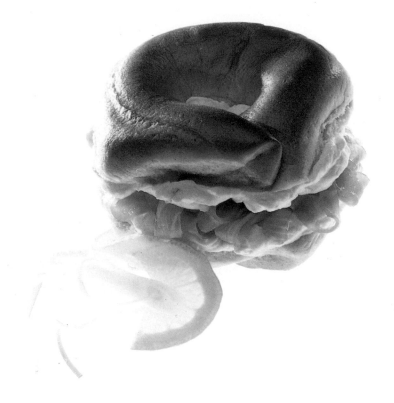

Smoked Salmon Bagels

2 plain bagels
2 (3-oz.) pkgs. cream cheese
2 teaspoons fresh lemon juice
2 tablespoons dairy sour cream
3 green onions, chopped
Dash cayenne pepper
2 to 3 ozs. thinly sliced smoked salmon
Green onion flowers and lemon twists to
    garnish

Preheat oven to 350F (175C). Wrap
bagels in foil. Heat in preheated oven
15 minutes. Meanwhile, in a medium-
size bowl, combine cream cheese,
lemon juice, sour cream, green onions
and cayenne pepper. Roll smoked salmon in rolls; cut in thin slices. Cut
warmed bagels in half. Spread each cut
side with 1/2 of cream cheese mixture.
Arrange salmon slices on bottom halves
of bagels. Cover with top halves. Garnish with green onion flowers and
lemon twists. Makes 2 bagels.

Egg & Bacon Rolls

6 slices bacon
2 long crusty rolls
3 tablespoons butter, softened
Tomato relish or chili sauce
Chicory or red leaf lettuce leaves
2 small tomatoes, sliced
2 hard-cooked eggs, sliced
Salt and pepper to taste
1 tablespoon mayonnaise, if desired
Sprigs of fresh parsley to garnish

In a medium-size skillet, fry bacon until crisp. Drain on paper towels. Meanwhile, partially slice rolls lengthwise; do not cut through bottom crust. Open and spread each cut side with butter. Spoon a small amount of tomato relish along sides of rolls. Arrange chicory leaves along 1 side of rolls and tomato slices along other side. Place egg slices in an overlapping row next to tomato slices. Season with salt and pepper. Spread egg slices with mayonnaise, if desired. Top with bacon. Garnish with parsley. Makes 2 rolls.

Variation: Substitute slices of cooked cold sausage for bacon.

Pork-Celery Crunch

1 tablespoon mayonnaise
1 teaspoon Dijon-style mustard
1 stalk celery, chopped
1 to 2 teaspoons applesauce, if desired
Salt and pepper to taste
2 tablespoons butter, softened
2 large thick slices whole-wheat bread
1 crisp green lettuce leaf
2 to 3 slices cooked roast pork
Red onion rings
Celery leaves to garnish

In a small bowl, mix mayonnaise, mustard, celery and applesauce, if desired. Season with salt and pepper. Mix well. Butter bread. Place lettuce leaf on 1 slice of buttered bread. Add pork and spoon celery mixture over pork. Reserve several red onion rings. Cover celery mixture with remaining red onion rings. Top with remaining slice of buttered bread. Press together lightly. Cut diagonally in quarters. Garnish with reserved red onion rings and celery leaves. Makes 1 sandwich.

Variation: Substitute cold roast beef or corned beef for pork and applesauce.

Smoked Fish Sandwich

1/2 (8-oz.) pkg. cream cheese
2 teaspoons prepared horseradish
2 teaspoons chopped fresh chives
1/4 cup butter, softened
4 thick slices crusty poppy seed bread
6 ozs. smoked mackerel, skinned, boned,
   flaked in large pieces
8 thin red bell pepper rings
2 teaspoons fresh lemon juice
Pepper to taste
1/3 bunch fresh watercress

In a small bowl, combine cream cheese, horseradish and chives. Butter bread. Spread 2 slices of buttered bread with cream cheese mixture. Cover with mackerel, then bell pepper rings. Sprinkle with lemon juice and season with pepper. Reserve 2 sprigs of watercress. Arrange remaining watercress on bell pepper rings. Top with remaining slices of buttered bread. Press together firmly. Cut each sandwich in half. Garnish with reserved watercress. Makes 2 sandwiches.

Variations: Substitute smoked trout or cooked, boned and skinned kippered salmon or herring for mackerel.

Scotch Egg Rolls

1/2 lb. pork sausage
1 small onion, finely chopped
Salt and pepper to taste
2 hard-cooked eggs, peeled
1 tablespoon all-purpose flour
1 egg, beaten
3 tablespoons dry bread crumbs
Vegetable oil for deep frying
4 round rolls
1/3 cup butter, softened
Chicory leaves
2 large tomatoes, thinly sliced
2 tablespoons piccalilli or hot dog relish
Crisp bacon rolls, radish flowers and
    additional chicory leaves to garnish

Place sausage and onion in a medium-size bowl. Season with salt and pepper. Mix well. Divide sausage mixture in half. Roll hard-cooked eggs in flour and flour hands. Wrap eggs in sausage mixture to enclose completely. Dip in beaten egg and roll in bread crumbs. Press bread crumbs on firmly. Half-fill a deep saucepan with oil. Heat to 375F (190C) or until a 1-inch cube of day-old bread browns in 40 seconds. Fry eggs 6 minutes or until golden. Drain on paper towels and cool. Cut off tops of rolls. Butter tops. Cut a thin slice from bottoms of rolls; spread each cut side with butter. Scoop out centers of rolls large enough to place half an egg; discard centers. Spread center sections with butter. Cover buttered bottom slices with chicory leaves and tomato slices. Place center sections on bottoms. Cut eggs in half; press into centers of rolls. Spoon on piccalilli. Place buttered tops at an angle. To garnish, thread 4 wooden picks with bacon rolls, radish flowers and additional chicory leaves; push into each roll. Makes 4 rolls.

Peppered Salami-Slaw Sandwich

1/4 cup very finely shredded red cabbage
2 green onions, chopped
1 carrot, grated
1/3 cup fresh bean sprouts
2 tablespoons French dressing
1/4 cup butter, softened
4 thick slices whole-wheat or white bread
6 slices peppered salami
8 thin slices cucumber
1 large tomato, thinly sliced
Salt and pepper to taste
8 small tomato wedges and sprigs of
    fresh parsley to garnish

Rinse cabbage in cold water; drain well. In a medium-size bowl, combine cabbage, green onions, carrot, bean sprouts and dressing. Toss well. Butter bread. Arrange salami over 2 slices of buttered bread. Cover with cucumber and tomato slices. Season with salt and pepper. Spoon on cabbage mixture and top with remaining slices of buttered bread. Press together firmly. Cut sandwiches in half. To garnish, thread 4 wooden picks with tomato wedges and parsley; push into each half. Makes 2 sandwiches.

Variation: Substitute packaged shredded cabbage for red cabbage.

Tuna-Avocado Sandwich

1 (3-1/2-oz.) can tuna in oil, drained
2 green onions, chopped
2 tablespoons prepared tartar sauce
Salt and pepper to taste
1 ripe avocado
1 tablespoon fresh lemon juice
1/4 cup butter, softened
4 square slices light rye bread
Small lemon wedges, additional avocado
    slices and sprigs of fresh parsley
    to garnish

Flake tuna into a medium-size bowl. Add green onions and 1 tablespoon of tartar sauce. Season with salt and pepper. Mix well. Cut avocado in half; remove pit and peel. Cut avocado in slices and dip into lemon juice. Butter bread. Cover 2 slices of buttered bread with tuna mixture and arrange avocado slices on top. Spread with remaining tartar sauce. Season with salt and pepper. Cover with remaining slices of buttered bread. Press together firmly. Cut diagonally in half. Garnish with lemon wedges, additional avocado slices and parsley. Makes 2 sandwiches.

Pâté Salad Croissants

2 croissants
2 tablespoons butter, softened
1-1/2 ozs. Boursin cheese
6 small Romaine lettuce leaves
2 thick slices large tomato, cut in half
4 ozs. firm pâté, sliced
Salt and pepper to taste
2 crisp bacon rolls, 2 pitted black olives
   and 2 small lettuce leaves to garnish

Cut croissants 2/3 way through center, cutting from rounded side through to pointed side; do not cut through crust. Open slightly and spread both sides of each croissant lightly with butter.

Spread 1 side of each croissant with cheese. Place lettuce leaves at an angle. Add half a tomato slice to each croissant. Arrange slices of pâté along 1 side of each croissant. Place remaining halved tomato slices along other side of pâté. Season with salt and pepper. To garnish, thread 2 wooden picks with bacon rolls, black olives and lettuce leaves; push into each croissant. Makes 2 croissants.

Variation: Top filled croissants with a small amount of mayonnaise or pickle.

Frankfurter Salad Sandwich

2 to 3 tablespoons potato salad
2 green onions, chopped
3 radishes, finely chopped
Salt and pepper to taste
3 tablespoons butter, softened
2 thick slices whole-wheat bread
1 teaspoon German or sweet mustard
2 frankfurters, cut diagonally in slices
8 thin cucumber slices
Green onion flowers and radish flowers
to garnish

In a small bowl, combine potato salad, green onions and radishes. Season with salt and pepper. Mix well. Butter bread. Spread 1 slice of buttered bread with mustard. Cover with frankfurter slices. Spoon potato salad mixture over frankfurters. Smooth surface. Top with cucumber slices. Season with salt and pepper. Place remaining slice of buttered bread on top. Press together lightly. Cut diagonally in half. Garnish with green onion and radish flowers. Makes 1 sandwich.

Bierwurst-Cheese Stack

1/4 cup butter, softened
2 large slices white bread, crusts
   removed
1 large slice whole-wheat bread, crust
   removed
1 carrot, grated
2 teaspoons chopped chives
1 tablespoon Thousand Island dressing
3 slices Bierwurst or bologna, rinds
   removed
1 medium-size tomato, thinly sliced
Salt and pepper to taste
1-1/2 ozs. red-veined Cheddar cheese,
   sliced
2 or 3 red leaf lettuce leaves
4 carrot curls and additional chopped
   chives to garnish

Butter white bread on 1 side and whole-wheat bread on both sides. In a small bowl, combine carrot, chives and 1 teaspoon of dressing. Spread carrot mixture on 1 slice of buttered white bread. Top with Bierwurst. Arrange tomato slices over Bierwurst. Sprinkle with 1 teaspoon of dressing. Season with salt and pepper. Cover with buttered whole-wheat bread. Arrange cheese slices on top. Cover with lettuce leaves. Spread remaining slice of buttered white bread with remaining dressing; place on lettuce leaves. Press together firmly. Cut diagonally in quarters. To garnish, thread 4 wooden picks with carrot curls; push into each quarter. Sprinkle with additional chopped chives. Makes 1 sandwich.

Variation: Substitute sliced salami, ham or garlic sausage for Bierwurst. Substitute blue cheese dressing, yogurt or mayonnaise for Thousand Island dressing.

Toasted Club Sandwich

2 large medium-thick slices white bread
1 large medium-thick slice whole-wheat
   bread
3 tablespoons butter, softened
2 ozs. sliced cooked chicken breast
1 medium-size tomato, sliced
8 thin slices cucumber
Salt and pepper to taste
1 tablespoon mayonnaise
1 hard-cooked egg, peeled, sliced
4 cocktail gherkin pickle fans and 4
   cocktail onions to garnish

Toast bread. Cut off crusts and stand upright to cool. Butter white bread on 1 side and whole-wheat bread on both sides. Cover 1 slice of buttered white bread with chicken and 1/2 of tomato and cucumber slices. Season with salt and pepper. Spread with 1/2 of mayonnaise. Top with buttered whole-wheat bread. Arrange remaining tomato and cucumber slices and egg slices on buttered whole-wheat bread. Season with salt and pepper. Spread with remaining mayonnaise. Top with remaining slice of buttered white bread. Press together firmly. Cut diagonally in triangles. To garnish, thread 4 wooden picks with pickle fans and cocktail onions; push into each triangle. Makes 1 sandwich.

Variation: Substitute sliced cheese for egg.

Liverwurst & Bacon Sandwich

4 strips bacon
1/4 cup butter, softened
2 large slices whole-wheat bread
1 large slice white bread
2 ozs. liverwurst, sliced
1 tablespoon mayonnaise
6 small Belgian endive leaves
Salt and pepper to taste
Tomato relish or chili sauce
4 green bell pepper rings
Sprigs of fresh parsley to garnish

In a medium-size skillet, fry bacon until crisp. Drain on paper towels. Butter whole-wheat bread on 1 side and white bread on both sides. Arrange liverwurst on 1 slice of buttered whole-wheat bread. Spread with mayonnaise. Top with endive leaves. Season with salt and pepper. Top with buttered white bread. Spread with tomato relish. Add bell pepper rings and top with bacon. Cover with remaining slice of buttered whole-wheat bread. Press together firmly. Cut diagonally in half. Garnish with parsley sprigs. Makes 1 sandwich.

Turkey & Ham Sandwich

3 tablespoons butter, softened
3 slices crusty seeded bread
2 to 3 ozs. sliced cooked turkey breast
Salt and pepper to taste
2 tablespoons cranberry sauce
4 small Romaine lettuce leaves
1 teaspoon mild mustard
1 tablespoon mayonnaise
2 slices cooked ham
3 radicchio leaves, finely shredded
Sprigs of fresh watercress to garnish

Butter 2 slices of bread on 1 side and remaining slice on both sides. Place turkey on 1 slice of bread buttered on 1 side. Season with salt and pepper. Spread cranberry sauce on turkey. Top with lettuce leaves. Cover with slice of bread buttered on both sides. In a small bowl, mix mustard and mayonnaise. Spread on ham. Roll up ham and cut in slices. Place on buttered bread. Top with shredded radicchio. Season with salt and pepper. Cover with remaining slice of buttered bread. Press together firmly. Cut in quarters. Garnish with watercress. Makes 1 sandwich.

Four Seasons Sandwich

3 large slices whole-wheat or white bread
1 tablespoon corn oil
2 ozs. small mushrooms, cut in thick
    slices
3 tablespoons butter, softened
1 teaspoon tomato paste
1 teaspoon chopped fresh marjoram
3 slices salami, rinds removed
2 ozs. sliced mozzarella cheese
Chicory leaves
1 thick slice large tomato
Salt and pepper to taste
4 pickled chilies and additional chicory
    leaves to garnish

Toast bread. Cut off crusts and stand upright to cool. Heat oil in a small skillet. Add mushrooms and saute gently 3 minutes. Drain on paper towels and cool. In a small bowl, mix butter, tomato paste and marjoram. Spread butter mixture on 1 side of 2 slices of bread and on both sides of remaining slice of bread. Cover 1 slice of bread buttered on 1 side with salami. Add cheese. Top with chicory leaves. Cover with slice of bread buttered on both sides. Arrange mushrooms on buttered bread and top with tomato slice. Season with salt and pepper. Cover with remaining slice of buttered bread. Press together firmly. Cut diagonally in quarters. To garnish, thread 4 wooden picks with chilies and additional chicory leaves; push into each quarter. Makes 1 sandwich.

———— Roast Beef Sandwich ————

2 tablespoons butter, softened
2 thick slices crusty white or whole-
  wheat bread
3 or 4 slices cooked rare roast beef
1 teaspoon prepared creamed
  horseradish
1/2 dill pickle, cut in lengthwise slices
1/2 small red onion, thinly sliced, then
  separated in rings
Chicory leaves
Salt and pepper to taste
2 to 3 teaspoons Thousand Island
  dressing
2 green onion flowers and 2 radish
  flowers to garnish

Butter bread. Cover 1 slice of buttered bread with roast beef, folding slices to fit bread. Spread roast beef with horse-radish. Arrange dill pickle slices and onion rings over roast beef. Top with chicory leaves. Season with salt and pepper. Spread remaining slice of but-tered bread with dressing. Place on chicory leaves. Press together firmly. Cut diagonally in half. Garnish with green onion flowers and radish flowers. Makes 1 sandwich.

— Bacon, Lettuce & Tomato Sandwich —

8 slices bacon
4 large medium-thick slices white bread
3 tablespoons mayonnaise
4 thick slices large tomato
Salt and pepper to taste
2 crisp lettuce leaves
Sprigs of fresh parsley to garnish

In a large skillet, fry bacon until crisp.
Drain on paper towels. Meanwhile,
toast bread. Cut off crusts, if desired.
Spread toast with mayonnaise. Arrange
tomato slices on 2 slices of toast. Season
with salt and pepper. Top with bacon
and lettuce leaves. Cover with remaining slices of toast. Cut diagonally in
quarters. Garnish with parsley. Makes 2
sandwiches.

‾Pickled Herring, Onion & Egg Sandwich‾

4 ozs. pickled herring, drained
1 tablespoon dairy sour cream
1/2 small red onion, thinly sliced
1/4 crisp Green Delicious apple, cored,
    thinly sliced
Salt and pepper to taste
4 slices light rye bread
2 slices dark rye bread
1/4 cup butter, softened
Sprigs of fresh watercress
2 hard-cooked eggs, sliced
1/2 bunch cress
Tomato wedges to garnish

Pat pickled herring dry on paper towels. Cut in thin slivers. In a medium-size bowl, combine pickled herring slivers, sour cream, onion and apple. Season with salt and pepper. Mix well. Cut bread slices to same size, if necessary. Butter slices of light rye bread on 1 side and dark rye bread on both sides. Spread 2 slices of buttered light rye bread with pickled herring mixture. Reserve 2 sprigs of watercress. Top pickled herring mixture with remaining watercress. Cover with slices of buttered dark rye bread. Arrange egg slices on dark rye bread. Season with salt and pepper. Sprinkle liberally with cress. Top with remaining slices of buttered light rye bread. Press together firmly. Cut diagonally in half. Garnish with reserved watercress and tomato wedges. Makes 2 sandwiches.

Double Cheese Decker Sandwich

3 slices crusty poppy seed bread
1/3 cup butter, softened
1 tablespoon corn relish
2 ozs. Red Leicester cheese, sliced
Red bell pepper rings
2 pickled onions, sliced
1/3 bunch fresh watercress
Salt and pepper to taste
3 radicchio leaves, finely shredded
2 teaspoons French dressing
2 ozs. Emmentaler cheese, sliced

Toast bread. In a small bowl, mix butter and corn relish. Spread butter mixture on 1 side of 2 slices of toast and on both sides of remaining slice of toast. Place Red Leicester cheese on 1 slice of toast buttered on 1 side. Reserve several bell pepper rings. Top with remaining bell pepper rings and pickled onion slices. Reserve several sprigs of watercress. Cover with remaining watercress. Season with salt and pepper. Top with slice of toast buttered on both sides. In a medium-size bowl, toss shredded radicchio in dressing. Spread on buttered toast. Top with Emmentaler cheese. Cover with remaining slice of buttered toast. Press together firmly. Cut in 3 thick pieces. Garnish with reserved bell pepper rings and reserved watercress. Makes 1 sandwich.

Stilton-Pear Topper

1-1/2 teaspoons unsalted butter, softened
1 slice crusty whole-wheat bread
Chicory leaves
2 slices Stilton cheese
1/2 ripe pear, cored, sliced
1 teaspoon lemon juice
1 large walnut half
Lemon twist and sprigs of fresh
**   watercress to garnish**

Butter bread. Place chicory leaves on
buttered bread. Press down lightly.
Place cheese on top of bread. Brush
pear slices with lemon juice; arrange in
an overlapping fan-shape on 1 side of
cheese. Add walnut half. Garnish with
lemon twist and watercress. Makes 1
sandwich.

Variation: Substitute Danish Blue,
Cambozola, Dolcelatte or Roquefort
cheese for Stilton cheese. Substitute
star fruit slices for pear slices.

Potted Shrimp Treat

3 tablespoons plus 1-1/2 teaspoons
   unsalted butter
2 ozs. peeled fresh shrimp, coarsely
   chopped
1/2 small clove garlic, crushed
1/8 teaspoon ground cumin
1/8 teaspoon ground mace
1/8 teaspoon cayenne pepper
1 teaspoon finely chopped fresh parsley
Salt and white pepper to taste
1 slice pumpernickel bread
3 or 4 small radicchio leaves
Sprigs of fresh flat-leafed parsley
1 peeled cooked shrimp to garnish

In a small saucepan, melt 1 tablespoon of butter. Add chopped shrimp and garlic. Cook gently 1 minute. Remove from heat and stir in cumin, mace, cayenne pepper and chopped parsley. Season with salt and white pepper. Mix well. Spoon mixture into a 1/2-cup ramekin. Smooth surface. Wash saucepan. Melt 2 tablespoons of butter in saucepan. Cool slightly, then pour over shrimp mixture. Cool and refrigerate 2 hours or until set. Spread remaining butter over bread. Top with radicchio leaves. Run a knife around edge of ramekin to loosen shrimp mold. Invert and remove shrimp mold. Place in center of bread. Arrange parsley around mold. Garnish with peeled shrimp. Makes 1 sandwich.

Spiced Egg Slice

1 hard-cooked egg, peeled, chopped
1 tablespoon mayonnaise
1 oz. Cheddar cheese, finely diced
1 green onion, chopped
1/2 to 3/4 teaspoon concentrated curry
    paste or 1 teaspoon curry powder
    plus 1 teaspoon mayonnaise
Salt and pepper to taste
1-1/2 teaspoons butter, softened
1 slice pumpernickel bread
16 thin cucumber slices
2 radish flowers and sprigs of fresh mint
    to garnish

In a small bowl, mix hard-cooked egg, mayonnaise, Cheddar cheese, green onion and curry paste. Season with salt and pepper. Butter bread. Arrange overlapping slices of cucumber around edge of buttered bread, allowing slices to slightly overlap edges of bread. Spoon curried egg mixture into center. Smooth slightly to cover inner edges of cucumber slices. Garnish with radish flowers and mint. Makes 1 sandwich.

Variation: Substitute dairy sour cream for mayonnaise and 1 tablespoon chopped chives for green onion.

Beef & Endive Crunch

1-1/2 teaspoons unsalted butter, softened
1 slice pumpernickel bread
4 or 5 Belgian endive leaves
1 teaspoon mayonnaise
1 teaspoon prepared creamed
 horseradish
2 slices cooked rare roast beef
1 tablespoon pickled red cabbage,
 drained
Sprigs of fresh dill and cucumber twists
 to garnish

Butter bread. Arrange endive leaves at an angle over buttered bread. In a small bowl, mix mayonnaise and creamed horseradish. Spread on slices of beef. Fold beef slices and place on endive leaves. Spoon on red cabbage. Garnish with dill and cucumber twists. Makes 1 sandwich.

Variation: Substitute slices of cooked ham or tongue for rare roast beef. Substitute shredded radicchio leaves, tossed in French dressing, for pickled red cabbage.

———— Goujons of Plaice Tartare ————

1 flounder fillet, skinned, boned, cut in
  very thin strips
1 teaspoon all-purpose flour
Salt and pepper to taste
1 small egg, beaten
2 to 3 tablespoons dry bread crumbs
Vegetable oil for frying
1-1/2 teaspoons unsalted butter, softened
1 slice dark rye bread, cut diagonally in
  half
1 large crisp lettuce leaf
4 red bell pepper rings
1/2 teaspoon lemon juice
Small lemon wedges and sprigs of fresh
  parsley to garnish
1 tablespoon prepared tartar sauce

Coat fish strips with flour. Season with
salt and pepper. Dip strips into beaten
egg. Coat in bread crumbs. Heat oil in a
small skillet. Fry fish strips 2 to 3 minutes or until golden brown and cooked
through. Drain on paper towels and
cool. Butter bread. Place lettuce leaf on
buttered bread. Arrange bell pepper
rings over lettuce. Mound fish strips on
top. Season with salt and pepper.
Sprinkle with lemon juice. If desired,
cut in half diagonally. Garnish with
lemon wedges and parsley. Serve with
tartar sauce. Makes 1 sandwich.

Brie & Fig Tempter

1-1/2 teaspoons unsalted butter, softened
1 rye crispbread or Scandinavian
**   flatbread**
2 or 3 small red leaf lettuce leaves
3 thin slices Brie cheese
1 fresh ripe fig, cut in 6 wedges
1 teaspoon fresh lime juice
Lime twists to garnish

Butter crispbread. Cover with lettuce leaves. Press down lightly. Arrange overlapping slices of cheese at a slight angle over lettuce leaves allowing ends to slightly overlap edges. Sprinkle fig wedges with lime juice. Arrange attractively with cheese. Garnish with lime twists. Makes 1 sandwich.

Variation: Substitute light or dark rye bread, sliced diagonally, for crispbread. Substitute sliced kiwifruit for fig.

Danish Herring on Rye

1-1/2 teaspoons unsalted butter, softened
1 slice light or dark rye bread, cut
diagonally in half
3 or 4 small Romaine lettuce leaves
Salt and pepper to taste
2 ozs. pickled herring, drained
1/4 crisp Red Delicious apple, cored,
thinly sliced
2 teaspoons lemon juice
Small onion rings, lemon twist and
sprigs of fresh dill to garnish

Butter bread. Arrange lettuce leaves diagonally on buttered bread allowing
leaf tips to overlap edges of bread. Press
leaves down firmly in center to flatten
slightly. Season with salt and pepper.
Place pickled herring in center. Brush
apple slices with lemon juice and arrange around pickled herring. Garnish
with onion rings, lemon twist and dill.
Makes 1 sandwich.

Variation: Substitute thin slivers of red
and green bell pepper for apples.

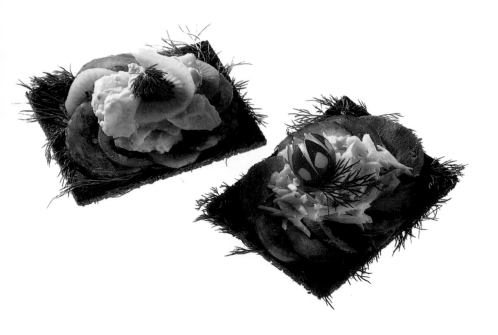

Tongue Petal Salad Sandwich

1-1/2 teaspoons unsalted butter, softened
1 slice pumpernickel bread
Sprigs of fresh dill
1 slice cooked beef tongue
3 thin slices cucumber
3 slices tomato
1-1/2 tablespoons coleslaw
Radish flowers to garnish

Butter bread. Reserve 2 sprigs of dill. Cover edges of bread with remaining dill allowing dill to overlap edges of bread. Using a 2-inch round cutter, cut 3 rounds from beef tongue. Arrange overlapping rounds of tongue in a

petal-like design over bread. Place cucumber and tomato slices between tongue rounds to give an attractive "flower" pattern. Spoon coleslaw into center. Garnish with reserved sprigs of dill and radish flowers. Makes 1 sandwich.

Variation: Substitute any cooked cold meat, such as ham, salami or bologna, for cooked tongue. Substitute thin slices of kiwifruit for cucumber and top with Waldorf salad or potato salad instead of coleslaw.

Ham & Asparagus Special

6 frozen asparagus spears
1-1/2 teaspoons unsalted butter, softened
1 slice pumpernickel bread
1/4 bunch cress
2 slices cooked ham
1 small tomato, cut in wedges
Mayonnaise and paprika to garnish

Cook asparagus spears following package directions. Drain, pat dry on paper towels and cool. Butter bread. Arrange cress around edges of bread. Cut ham in 2 (3-inch) squares. Place 3 asparagus spears diagonally across each square of ham. Trim stalks, if necessary. Fold sides to middle. Secure with wooden picks. Arrange ham and asparagus "envelopes" at an angle over buttered bread. Add tomato wedges. Garnish with piped mayonnaise and sprinkle with paprika. Makes 1 sandwich.

Note: Canned asparagus spears may be used, although the color is not as bright.

— Avocado-Shrimp Cocktail Sandwich —

2 tablespoons French dressing
2 ozs. peeled cooked fresh or frozen
   shrimp, thawed if frozen
1-1/2 teaspoons unsalted butter, softened
1 slice pumpernickel bread
Sprigs of fresh watercress
1/2 small ripe avocado
2 teaspoons fresh lemon juice
Salt and pepper to taste
2 tablespoon mayonnaise
Sprigs of fresh dill and lemon peel curls
   to garnish

In a small bowl, whisk dressing. Add shrimp. Stir well. Cover and refrigerate 1 hour, stirring occasionally. Drain shrimp. Butter bread. Arrange watercress on buttered bread, slightly overlapping watercress on edges of bread. Peel avocado, cut in thin slices lengthwise and dip into lemon juice. Arrange avocado slices over watercress. Season with salt and pepper. Arrange diagonal rows of shrimp over avocado slices. Using a pastry bag fitted with a small star tube, pipe mayonnaise between rows of shrimp. Garnish with dill and lemon peel. Makes 1 sandwich.

Salami Sandwich

1-1/2 teaspoons unsalted butter, softened
1 slice light rye bread, cut diagonally in
    half
2 slices green peppercorn salami or
    pistachio Mortadella
3 or 4 radishes, sliced
1 tablespoon French dressing
4 pitted black olives
Gherkin pickle fan and sprigs of fresh
    cilantro to garnish

Butter bread. Cut slices of salami in half. Form each half in a cone shape. Place cones joined-side down on buttered bread, slightly overlapping. Dip radish slices into dressing. Arrange in overlapping rows over remaining area of buttered bread. Place an olive in each salami cone. Garnish with pickle fan and cilantro. Makes 1 sandwich.

Variation: Pipe softened cream cheese into salami cones. Sprinkle with a few snipped chives.

Note: To make a pickle fan, cut 3 or 4 (1/8-inch) slices from stalk end through to pointed ends of a small gherkin pickle. Carefully open slices to form a fan.

— Roquefort Grape Relish Sandwich —

1-1/2 teaspoons unsalted butter, softened
1 slice dark rye bread, cut diagonally in
**   half**
Green lettuce leaves
2 or 3 slices Roquefort cheese
2 or 3 sprigs seedless black or green
**   grapes**
2 teaspoons dairy sour cream
Lime twists and sprigs of fresh chervil
**   to garnish**

Butter bread. Cover buttered bread
with lettuce leaves allowing tips of
leaves to overlap edges of bread. Arrange overlapping slices of cheese over
lettuce. Place grapes on 1 side and
spoon sour cream on other side. Garnish with lime twists and chervil. Makes
1 sandwich.

Variation: Substitute Gorgonzolia
cheese for Roquefort cheese and sprigs
of watercress for green lettuce leaves.
Substitute mayonnaise for dairy sour
cream.

Gravlax Slice

1-1/2 teaspoons unsalted butter, softened
1 slice light rye bread, cut diagonally
in half
12 large watercress leaves
2 ozs. sliced Gravlax
3 cucumber twists
2 teaspoons dairy sour cream
1/2 teaspoon wholegrain mustard
Sprigs of fresh dill to garnish

Butter bread. Arrange watercress leaves around edge of buttered bread to form a border, allowing leaves to overlap edges of bread. Arrange slices of Gravlax over buttered bread. Place cucumber twists across 1 end. In a small bowl, mix sour cream and mustard. Spoon onto sandwich in a swirl. Garnish with dill. Makes 1 sandwich.

Variation: Substitute thinly sliced smoked salmon, rolled, for Gravlax. Garnish with lemon wedges, fresh chervil and black lumpfish caviar.

Note: Gravlax is pickled fresh salmon flavored with dill. It is now widely available, fresh or frozen, from delicatessens and specialty food markets.

Italian Special

1-1/2 teaspoons unsalted butter, softened
1 slice light or dark rye bread, cut
   diagonally in half
2 or 3 small red or green leaf lettuce
   leaves
2 slices prosciutto
2 or 3 thin slices mozzarella cheese
2 or 3 tomato slices
2 or 3 pitted black or green olives
1/2 teaspoon olive oil
1/2 teaspoon chopped fresh basil
Freshly ground pepper to taste
Sprigs of fresh basil to garnish

Butter bread. Cover buttered bread with lettuce leaves. Roll proscuitto in cone shaped rolls. Place rolls slightly to 1 side at a slight angle over lettuce leaves. Arrange an overlapping border of alternating cheese and tomato slices in front of rolls. Place olives in center of rolls. Drizzle olive oil over cheese and tomato slices, then sprinkle with chopped basil. Season with pepper. Garnish with sprigs of basil. Makes 1 sandwich.

Variation: Substitute slices of salami, mortadella or bologna cut in half for prosciutto.

Mango & Crab Sandwich

1-1/2 teaspoons unsalted butter, softened
1 slice dark rye bread, cut diagonally
in half
2 ozs. white crabmeat
1 green onion, finely chopped
3 tablespoon mayonnaise
3 drops hot-pepper sauce
Few drops fresh lemon juice
Salt and pepper to taste
Chicory leaves
1/2 small ripe mango, pitted, peeled, cut
in thin slivers
1 or 2 green onion flowers and lemon
slices, cut in quarters, to garnish

Butter bread. Flake crabmeat into a small bowl. Add green onion, 2 teaspoons of mayonnaise, hot-pepper sauce and lemon juice to flaked crabmeat. Season with salt and pepper. Mix well. Cover buttered bread with chicory leaves. Spoon crab mixture onto center of chicory leaves. Arrange mango around crab mixture. In a pastry bag fitted with a small star tube, pipe a rosette with remaining mayonnaise on 2 opposite corners of sandwich. Garnish with green onion flowers and lemon slices. Makes 1 sandwich.

Egg & Anchovy Salad Sandwich

1-1/2 teaspoons unsalted butter, softened
1 slice crusty poppy seed bread
2 ozs. cream cheese, softened
1 tablespoon mayonnaise
1/2 teaspoon tomato paste
Salt and pepper to taste
1 small green leaf lettuce leaf
1 hard-boiled egg, peeled, sliced
5 or 6 anchovy fillets, drained, patted
    dry, rolled
6 or 7 thin red bell pepper strips
Paprika
Sprigs of fresh watercress to garnish

Butter bread. In a small bowl, mix cream cheese, mayonnaise and tomato paste until soft and well combined. Season with salt and pepper. Mix well. Spoon 3/4 of cream cheese mixture into lettuce leaf. Spread remainder over buttered bread. Arrange overlapping egg slices over crusty top and down 1 side of buttered bread. Place filled lettuce leaf in remaining space. Arrange rolled anchovy fillets around edge of cream cheese mixture in lettuce leaf. Place bell pepper strips around edge of each egg slice. Sprinkle paprika on cream cheese mixture. Garnish with watercress. Makes 1 sandwich.

Chili Dogs

3 tablespoons corn oil
1 small onion, thinly sliced
1 garlic clove, crushed
1 teaspoon chili powder
1 (8-oz.) can tomatoes, drained, chopped
1 tablespoon tomato paste
1/2 teaspoon dry mustard
1 tablespoon malt vinegar
1 tablespoon Worcestershire sauce
1 tablespoon soft light-brown sugar
1/4 teaspoon salt
1 (8-oz.) can barbecue beans
4 frankfurters
4 seeded hotdog rolls
1/4 cup butter, softened
Onion rings
Snipped green onion stems and fresh
    cress to garnish

To prepare chili sauce, heat 2 table-spoons of oil in a medium-size sauce-pan. Add onion, garlic and chili powder; saute 2 minutes. Stir in toma-toes, tomato paste, dry mustard, malt vinegar, Worcestershire sauce, brown sugar and salt. Simmer 5 minutes. Stir in beans; cook 5 minutes. Meanwhile, preheat broiler. Cut frankfurters alter-nately on both sides at 1/2-inch in-tervals. Brush with remaining oil. Broil under preheated broiler 3 to 4 minutes or until browned, turning frequently. Cut rolls lengthwise, but do not cut through. Open and spread with butter. Place frankfurters in rolls. Arrange on-ion rings along 1 side of each frankfurt-er. Spoon chili sauce over frankfurters. Garnish with green onion stems and cress. Makes 4 chili dogs.

Chilied Salami Hero

1/2 long French bread roll
3 tablespoons butter, softened
1 small garlic clove, crushed
1 to 2 tablespoons canned chopped green
    chilies
1/2 ripe avocado
1 teaspoon fresh lemon juice
4 slices salami, rinds removed
1 slice processed Cheddar cheese
Cherry tomatoes and pickled whole
    chilies to garnish

Cut roll lengthwise 2/3 way from bottom to top; do not cut through top crust. Open roll and remove center. In a small bowl, mix butter and garlic. Butter inside of roll. Sprinkle bottom of roll with chopped chilies. Peel avocado, cut in thin slices and dip into lemon juice. Arrange avocado slices along bottom of roll in a fan-shape. Fold salami slices in quarters. Arrange over avocado slices. Cut cheese slice diagonally in quarters and arrange along other side of roll. To garnish, thread 2 or 3 wooden picks with cherry tomatoes and pickled whole chilies; push into roll. Makes 1 sandwich.

Ham & Cheese Roll-Ups

1 thin loaf sesame seed French bread
1/4 cup butter, softened
1 teaspoon prepared mustard
2 to 3 tablespoons mayonnaise
3 square slices cooked ham
8 ozs. ricotta cheese
1 bunch cress, snipped
Salt and pepper to taste
18 thin slices cucumber
3 small tomatoes, thinly sliced
Sprigs of fresh watercress to garnish

Using a sharp knife, cut out 6 "V" shaped pieces at regular intervals along bread, deep and wide enough to hold a stuffed ham roll and cucumber and tomato slices. In a small bowl, mix butter and mustard. Spread butter mixture inside "V" shapes, then spread with mayonnaise. Spread ham slices with ricotta cheese. Arrange snipped cress, green parts facing outwards, along 2 opposite edges. Season with salt and pepper. Roll up ham to show green cress at ends. Cut each ham roll in half. Arrange overlapping cucumber and tomato slices in each "V" shaped cut. Place a ham roll in each "V" shape. Garnish with watercress. Cut in 6 thick slices. Makes 6 pieces.

Pizza-Style Kebabs

1/4 cup plus 1 tablespoons olive oil
1 large onion, finely chopped
2 garlic cloves, crushed
1-1/2 teaspoons dried leaf oregano
1 (6-oz.) can tomato paste
Salt and pepper to taste
4 ozs. mozzarella cheese
4 ozs. (1/2-inch-thick) ham or salami, cut
   in 1/2-inch cubes
1 small green bell pepper, seeded, cut in
   1/2-inch pieces
8 small mushrooms, cut in half
2 teaspoons active dry yeast
1-1/4 cups warm (120F/45C) water
4 cups all-purpose flour
1/2 teaspoon salt
1 beaten egg
Sea salt
Sprigs of fresh oregano to garnish

To make sauce, heat olive oil in a medium-size saucepan. Add onion and garlic; saute 3 minutes. Stir in dried oregano and tomato paste. Season with salt and pepper. Mix well and cool.

Grease a baking sheet. Cut 2/3 of cheese in 1/2-inch cubes. Grate remaining cheese. Thread cubes of cheese and ham, bell pepper and mushrooms onto 4 (12- to 14-inch) bamboo skewers, leaving 1 inch clear on each end. In a large bowl, dissolve yeast in 1/4 cup of warm water. Let stand until bubbly. Add remaining warm water, flour and salt. Mix to a soft dough. If needed, add more warm water. Knead well; divide in 4 equal pieces. Roll each piece to a 10-inch circle. Spread with sauce to within 1/2 inch of edge. Place kebabs on edges of circles and roll up. Place on greased baking sheet. Brush with egg. Sprinkle with grated cheese and sea salt. Cover with oiled plastic wrap. Let stand in a warm place 20 minutes or until slightly puffy. Meanwhile, pre-heat oven to 350F (175C). Bake in pre-heated oven 20 to 25 minutes or until golden. Remove skewers. Cut each kebab in 3 pieces. Garnish with fresh oregano. Makes 4 kebabs.

Cheesy Garlic Bread

1 short loaf French bread
1/2 cup butter, softened
1 or 2 garlic cloves, crushed
1 tablespoon chopped fresh herbs
  (chives, parsley, chervil)
1 teaspoon fresh lemon juice
1/2 cup grated Red Leicester or Cheddar
  cheese
4 slices cooked ham, cut in quarters
Sprigs of fresh herbs to garnish

Preheat oven to 375F (190C). Cut bread in 4 equal pieces. Cut each piece in 4 thick slices; do not to cut through bottom crust. In a small bowl, mix butter, garlic, chopped herbs, lemon juice and 1/2 of cheese until well combined.

Spread cheese mixture between each slice of bread and at each cut end, reserving a small amount to spread on tops. Fold ham quarters and place between bread slices. Place pieces of bread on individual pieces of foil. Butter top of each with remaining butter mixture. Enclose each piece tightly in foil. Bake in preheated oven 15 minutes. Open foil and sprinkle with remaining cheese. Return to oven and bake 6 minutes or until cheese melts. Garnish with herbs and serve hot. Makes 4 pieces.

Variation: Substitute garlic sausage or salami for ham.

Hummus Salad Bread Loaf

1/2 (15-1/2-oz.) can garbanzo beans, drained
2 garlic cloves
2 tablespoons olive oil
1 tablespoon tahini (creamed sesame)
2 tablespoons fresh lemon juice
1/8 teaspoon cayenne pepper
1/4 to 1/2 teaspoon ground cumin
1/2 teaspoon salt
2 tablespoons chopped fresh parsley
Pepper to taste
1 short loaf sesame seed French bread
1/4 cup butter, softened
1 red bell pepper, seeded, cut in rings
1/2 Spanish onion, sliced thinly, then separated in rings
1 oz. fresh bean sprouts
2 Chinese cabbage leaves, shredded
2 tablespoons French dressing
Sprigs of fresh parsley to garnish

In a food processor fitted with the metal blade or a blender, process garbanzo beans, garlic, olive oil, tahini, lemon juice, cayenne pepper, cumin, salt and chopped parsley until smooth. Season with pepper and additional salt, if desired. Cut bread in half lengthwise. Butter both bread halves, then spread bottom half of buttered bread with garbanzo bean mixture. Cover with bell pepper and onion rings. In a small bowl, toss bean sprouts and shredded cabbage in dressing. Drain and spoon over bell pepper and onion rings. Cover with top half of buttered bread. With fine string, tie in 4 places to hold loaf together. Cut in 4 thick pieces. Garnish with sprigs of parsley: Makes 4 pieces.

Greek Salad Pitas

1/2 cup plus 2 tablespoons olive oil
2 tablespoons fresh lemon juice
1 garlic clove, crushed
1/4 teaspoon sugar
1 teaspoon chopped fresh oregano
Salt and pepper to taste
1/4 head Romaine lettuce, shredded
1 small red onion, sliced, then separated
   in rings
1/4 cucumber, thinly sliced
1 large tomato, cut in quarters, then
   sliced
1/2 small green bell pepper, seeded, cut
   in slivers
4 ozs. feta cheese, cut in cubes or fingers
4 large pita breads
12 pitted black olives
Lemon twists and sprigs of fresh Italian
   parsley to garnish

To make dressing, in a large bowl, whisk olive oil, lemon juice, garlic, sugar and oregano. Season with salt and pepper. Add shredded lettuce, onion, cucumber, tomato, bell pepper and cheese. Toss lightly until coated with dressing. Lightly toast pita breads. Cut a slice off long edge of each and open to form pockets. Generously fill each pita with salad mixture, allowing mixture to rise above top edges of breads. Add olives to each. Garnish with lemon twists and parsley. Makes 4 sandwiches.

Variation: Add peeled cooked shrimp to salad and toss with dressing.

Pita Lamb Keftadas

1 slice whole-wheat bread, crusts
  removed
1 tablespoon cold water
8 ozs. lean lamb, minced
1 small onion, finely chopped
2 tablespoons beaten egg
2 teaspoons fresh lemon juice
1/2 teaspoon dried leaf thyme
1/2 teaspoon dried leaf oregano
2 tablespoons chopped fresh mint
Salt and pepper to taste
Vegetable oil for frying
1/4 cucumber, sliced lengthwise, cut
  in strips
3 green onions, chopped
1/4 red bell pepper, seeded, chopped
2/3 cup plain yogurt
2 large pita breads
Lemon wedges and sprigs of fresh mint
  to garnish

In a medium-size bowl, soak bread in cold water 5 minutes, then crumble bread. Add lamb, onion, egg, 1 teaspoon of lemon juice, thyme, oregano and 1 tablespoon of chopped mint. Season with salt and pepper. Mix well. Using well-floured hands, form mixture in small balls the size of a walnut. Heat oil in a large skillet. Fry meatballs 10 to 12 minutes or until golden. Drain on paper towels. In a small bowl, combine cucumber, green onions and bell pepper. In another small bowl, mix yogurt with remaining lemon juice and mint. Season with salt and pepper. Mix well. Stir 2 tablespoons of yogurt mixture into cucumber mixture. Toast pita bread until warmed through. Cut a slice off long edge of each and open to form pockets. Spoon cucumber salad into pockets and fill with meatballs. Top with a small amount of yogurt mixture. Garnish with lemon wedges and sprigs of mint and serve hot with remaining yogurt sauce. Makes 2 sandwiches.

— Indian Spiced Chicken on Nan Bread —

1 small eggplant, trimmed, diced
1-1/2 teaspoons salt
1/4 cup corn oil
1 lb. skinned boneless chicken breasts,
   cut in thin strips
1 green bell pepper, seeded, diced
2 medium-size onions, cut in half, then
   thinly sliced
1 (2-inch) piece gingerroot, peeled, finely
   chopped
1 teaspoon ground cumin
1 teaspoon ground coriander
1/4 teaspoon turmeric
1/2 teaspoon chili powder
1/2 teaspoon ground cinnamon
2 garlic cloves, crushed
3 tablespoons plain yogurt
3 tablespoons cold water
2 nan breads
3 tablespoons butter, softened
2 tomatoes, peeled, seeded, cut in slivers
Sprigs of fresh cilantro to garnish

In a colander, layer eggplant with 1 teaspoon of salt. Drain over a plate 30 minutes. Rinse well and pat dry on paper towels. Heat 2 tablespoons of oil in a medium-size saucepan. Add chicken and stir-fry 3 minutes. Remove chicken from pan. Add remaining oil to pan. Heat oil and add eggplant, bell pepper, onions, gingerroot, spices and garlic. Stir-fry 3 minutes. Add chicken and stir in remaining salt, yogurt and cold water. Cover and cook 10 minutes, stirring occasionally. Meanwhile, toast breads until lightly golden and heated through. Butter bread. Cut each buttered bread in 2 or 3 serving pieces. Stir tomatoes into chicken mixture. Serve hot on buttered bread. Garnish with cilantro. Makes 4 to 6 pieces.

Pan Bagna

1/4 cup plus 2 tablespoons olive oil
2 tablespoons wine or malt vinegar
1 garlic clove, crushed
1/2 teaspoon Dijon-style mustard
1/2 teaspoon sugar
Salt and pepper to taste
1 short loaf French bread
1/4 head curly endive
4 medium-size tomatoes, sliced
8 green bell pepper rings
1 (6-oz.) can pimentos, drained, cut in
    thin strips
12 pitted black olives, cut in half
1 (2-oz.) can anchovy fillets, drained, cut
    in half lengthwise
1 tablespoon chopped fresh parsley
Sliced black olives and sprigs of fresh
    parsley to garnish

To make dressing, in a small bowl, whisk olive oil, wine vinegar, garlic, mustard and sugar. Season with salt and pepper. Mix until thoroughly combined. Cut bread in 4 pieces. Cut each piece in half lengthwise. Remove most of soft bread from each half. Brush with dressing. Arrange several endive leaves on bottom halves of bread. Dip tomatoes and bell pepper rings into remaining dressing and arrange over endive leaves. Arrange 1/2 of pimento strips over bell pepper rings. Top with halved olives and anchovy fillets. Sprinkle with chopped parsley. Cover with top halves of bread. Wrap each piece in foil. Place on a plate. Cover with another plate and weigh down with heavy weights. Refrigerate at least 1 hour before serving. Arrange remaining pimento strips in a crisscross pattern over tops of bread. Garnish with sliced olives and parsley. Makes 4 pieces.

New Orleans Oyster Loaf

12 fresh or bottled oysters
1/2 cup plus 2 tablespoons all-purpose
   flour
Salt and pepper to taste
1/8 teaspoon salt
3/8 teaspoon cayenne pepper
1 teaspoon corn oil
3 tablespoons cold water
1 egg white, beaten until stiff
Vegetable oil for deep frying
1 short loaf whole-wheat French bread
2/3 cup prepared tartar sauce
2 lettuce leaves, shredded
4 green onion flowers and lemon wedges
   to garnish

Pat oysters dry on paper towels. Dust
with 2 tablespoons of flour. Season with
salt and pepper. To make batter, in a
medium-size bowl, mix remaining
flour, 1/8 teaspoon salt, cayenne pepper, corn oil and cold water until thick.
Fold beaten egg white into batter. Half-
fill a deep saucepan with oil and heat to
375F (190C) or until 1 cube of day-old
bread browns in 40 seconds. Dip prepared oysters into batter. Deep-fry
oysters 3 to 4 minutes or until golden.
Drain on paper towels and keep warm.
Cut bread lengthwise 1/3 of way from
top; do not cut completely through bottom. Remove most of soft bread. Spoon
2/3 of tartar sauce into bottom half of
bread, spreading a small amount inside
top half. Fill bottom half of bread with
shredded lettuce. Season with salt and
pepper. Place oysters on lettuce. Spoon
remaining tartar sauce over oysters.
Garnish with green onion flowers and
lemon wedges. Cut in half and serve
hot. Makes 2 sandwiches.

Saucy Seafood Loaf

1 short loaf French bread
1/3 cup butter
1 medium-size onion, finely chopped
1/2 cup all-purpose flour
1-1/4 cups milk
1/2 cup half and half
2 tablespoons dry white wine
6 ozs. peeled cooked fresh or frozen
  shrimp, thawed if frozen
6 ozs. cooked salmon steak, page 16
2 tablespoons chopped fresh parsley
Salt and pepper to taste
1/4 cup grated Emmentaler or Cheddar
  cheese
Lemon slices, unpeeled cooked shrimp
  and sprigs of fresh parsley to garnish

Preheat oven to 375F (190C). Cut bread lengthwise along top; do not cut through bottom. Open slightly. Remove soft bread from both sides, leaving shell intact. Prepare 3 tablespoons bread crumbs from soft bread. Melt 1/4 cup of butter in a medium-size saucepan. Add onion; saute 3 minutes. Stir in flour. Cook 1 minute, then gradually stir in milk and half and half. Bring to a boil, stirring constantly. Simmer 2 minutes. Add wine, peeled shrimp, salmon and chopped parsley. Season with salt and pepper. Mix well. Spoon seafood mixture into bread shell. Place a sheet of foil on a baking sheet. Place filled bread shell on foil. Melt remaining butter in a small saucepan. Remove from heat and mix in bread crumbs. Sprinkle buttered bread crumbs over seafood mixture in bread shell. Sprinkle with cheese. Wrap foil around sides of loaf, leaving top exposed. Bake in preheated oven 20 to 25 minutes or until topping is golden. Garnish with lemon slices, unpeeled shrimp and parsley sprigs. Cut in 4 pieces and serve hot. Makes 4 pieces.

Steak Sandwich

3 tablespoons butter
1 thick slice crusty whole-wheat or
  white bread
1 medium-size onion, cut in half, then
  thinly sliced
1 garlic clove, crushed
1/4 lb. sirloin steak, cut in thin strips
2 tablespoons whipping cream
1 tablespoon water
1 teaspoon tomato paste
1 to 2 teaspoons chopped fresh chives
1/4 teaspoon prepared mustard
Salt and pepper to taste
Small onion rings and chives to garnish

Butter bread with 1 tablespoon of butter. Heat remaining butter in a medium-size skillet. Add onion; saute 2 minutes. Increase heat to medium high. Add garlic and steak. Fry until steak is cooked as desired, stirring frequently. Using a slotted spoon, remove steak and onion to a plate and keep warm. To prepare sauce, stir whipping cream, water, tomato paste, chopped chives and mustard into juices in skillet. Bring to a boil, stirring to scrape sediment in skillet. Season with salt and pepper. Simmer 30 seconds. Spoon steak and onions onto buttered bread and drizzle with sauce. Garnish with onion rings and chives. Serve at once. Makes 1 sandwich.

Chicken Chili Tacos

3 tablespoons corn oil
1 medium-size onion, chopped
1 garlic clove, crushed
1-1/2 teaspoons chili powder
1/2 teaspoon ground cumin
3/4 lb. skinned boneless chicken breast,
    finely chopped or minced
2 tablespoons tomato paste
1/2 (4-oz.) can chopped green chilies,
    drained
2/3 cup chicken stock
2 teaspoons cornstarch
1 tablespoon cold water
6 taco shells
Finely shredded lettuce leaves
Slivered onion
Chopped tomatoes
Sour cream

Preheat oven to 350F (175C). Heat oil in a medium-size skillet. Add onion, garlic, chili powder, cumin and chicken. Saute 4 to 5 minutes, stirring frequently. Stir in tomato paste, green chilies and chicken stock. Simmer 10 minutes, stirring occasionally. In a 1-cup glass measure, combine cornstarch and cold water. Stir into chicken mixture. Cook 2 minutes, stirring constantly. Meanwhile, heat taco shells in preheated oven following package directions. Fill hot taco shells with chicken mixture. Top with shredded lettuce, slivered onion and tomatoes. Add a dollop of sour cream. Serve at once. Makes 6 tacos.

Variation: Substitute lean ground beef or minced pork for chicken.

Leek & Ham Muffins

1/2 cup butter
1 large leek, cleaned, cut in thin slices
1/4 cup all-purpose flour
2/3 cup milk
3/4 cup grated Cheddar cheese
2 thin slices cooked ham, chopped
1/2 teaspoon prepared mustard
Salt and pepper to taste
3 plain muffins
Paprika
Sprigs of fresh parsley to garnish

Melt 2 tablespoons of butter in a medium-size saucepan. Add leek; saute lightly 3 minutes. Stir in flour and cook 1 minute. Add milk and bring to a boil, stirring constantly. Simmer 2 minutes or until thick, stirring constantly. Remove from heat and stir in 1/2 cup of cheese, ham and mustard. Season with salt and pepper. Mix well. Toast whole muffins on both sides until golden. Cut a thin slice off each muffin and reserve. Remove centers of muffins, leaving a 1/4-inch shell. Prepare fine crumbs from centers of muffins. Melt 2 tablespoons of butter in a small saucepan. Remove from heat and mix in crumbs. Cool, then mix with remaining cheese. Meanwhile, preheat broiler. Spread remaining butter over scooped out muffins and on cut sides of reserved slices. Fill bottoms with leek mixture and tops with crumb mixture. Broil under preheated broiler 5 minutes or until golden brown. Sprinkle reserved slices of muffin with paprika and cut in half to form "wings." With a knife, make an indentation in leek mixture and arrange "wings" on top. Garnish with a row of parsley sprigs. Makes 3 muffins.

Italian Meatball Hero

1 tablespoon olive oil
1 small onion, finely chopped
1 garlic clove, crushed
2 teaspoons dried leaf oregano
1 (8-oz.) can tomatoes, drained, chopped
1 tablespoon tomato paste
1 French roll
2/3 lb. lean ground beef
Salt and pepper to taste
Vegetable oil for frying
1/3 cup butter, softened
6 ozs. sliced mozzarella cheese
Sprigs of fresh watercress to garnish

To prepare tomato sauce, heat olive oil in a medium-size saucepan. Add onion, garlic, 1 teaspoon of oregano, tomatoes and tomato paste. Cook 10 minutes or until thick, stirring occasionally. Meanwhile, preheat oven to 375F (190C). Cut bread horizontally in half; do not cut through bottom crust. Remove all soft bread from center of both halves, leaving shell intact. Prepare 2 tablespoons of bread crumbs from soft bread. In a medium-size bowl, combine remaining bread crumbs and ground beef. Season with salt and pepper. Mix well. Form mixture in 12 small balls. Heat oil in a medium-size skillet. Add meatballs and fry 5 minutes or until set and golden. Drain on paper towels. Spread inside of bread shell with 2/3 of butter and add 1/2 of tomato sauce. Fill bread shell with meatballs and spoon sauce over meatballs. Cover with 1/2 of cheese slices. Press bread shell together. Spread outside of shell with remaining butter and cover with remaining slices of cheese and oregano. Wrap sandwich completely in greased foil. Bake in preheated oven 20 minutes. Unwrap foil to expose sandwich and bake 8 to 10 minutes more or until crisp. Cut in 4 thick pieces. Garnish with watercress. Makes 4 pieces.

Chicken Maryland Rolls

4 crusty poppy seed bowknot-shaped
   rolls
1/3 cup butter, softened
2 (4-oz.) skinned boneless chicken breasts
Salt and pepper to taste
1/2 cup all-purpose flour
1 egg
1 tablespoon milk
2 green onions, chopped
2 baking potatoes, grated
1/4 cup canned or frozen corn, thawed
   if frozen
Vegetable oil for shallow frying
2 small bananas
Green leaf lettuce leaves
Tomato relish
2 tomatoes, thinly sliced
Fresh cress to garnish

Cut rolls in half. Spread with 1/4 cup of
butter. Cut each chicken breast in 4 thin
slices, cutting at an angle. Season with
salt and pepper. In a large bowl, mix
flour, egg and milk. Add green onions,
potatoes and corn. Season with salt and
pepper. Mix well. Heat oil in a large
skillet. Divide potato mixture in 4 equal
portions. Press in patties the same size
as rolls. Fry patties 6 minutes or until
golden, turning once. Drain on paper
towels and keep warm. Pour oil from
skillet. Heat remaining butter in skillet.
Fry chicken slices 2 to 3 minutes on
each side. Drain on paper towels and
keep warm. Cut bananas in half crosswise and then in half lengthwise. Fry in
skillet 30 to 45 seconds. Spread tomato
relish on rolls, then top with lettuce
leaves. Place potato patties on lettuce
leaves. Add tomatoes, chicken and
bananas. Cover with top halves of rolls.
Secure with wooden picks. Garnish
with cress. Makes 4 rolls.

Ham & Pineapple Muffins

2 plain muffins, cut in half
2 tablespoons butter
4 (1/4-inch-thick) slices cooked ham
4 thick slices large tomato
4 canned pineapple slices, drained
1 tablespoon plus 1 teaspoon piccalilli or hot dog relish
1 cup grated Jarlsberg cheese
1/2 cup grated red-veined Cheddar cheese
Sprigs of fresh cilantro to garnish

Preheat broiler. Toast muffins. Spread with butter. Using a 3-1/2-inch round cutter, cut 4 rounds from slices of ham. Preheat broiler. Place ham rounds on buttered muffins. Top with tomato slices. Pat pineapple slices dry on paper towels; place on tomato slices. Spoon piccalilli into each pineapple center. In a small bowl, combine cheeses. Mound on pineapple. Broil under preheated broiler 6 to 7 minutes or until cheese is melted, bubbling and light golden. Garnish with cilantro. Makes 4 muffins.

Sesame Shrimp Fingers

4 ozs. fresh or frozen peeled cooked
   shrimp, thawed if frozen,
   coarsely chopped
1 (1/2-inch) piece gingerroot, peeled,
   grated
1 garlic clove, crushed
2 teaspoons light soy sauce
1 tablespoon ketchup
2 green onions, chopped
Pepper to taste
1/4 cup butter, softened
4 medium-thick slices white or
   whole-wheat bread, crusts removed
2 eggs, beaten
2 tablespoons milk
2 tablespoons sesame seeds
1 tablespoon corn oil
Unpeeled cooked shrimp, sprigs of fresh
   cilantro and slivers of green onion
   to garnish

In a medium-size bowl, combine shrimp, gingerroot, garlic, soy sauce, ketchup and chopped green onions. Season with pepper. Mix well. Butter bread with 1/2 of butter. Spread shrimp mixture on 2 slices of buttered bread. Cover with remaining slices of buttered bread. Press together firmly. In a small bowl, beat eggs and milk. Pour into a shallow dish. Dip sandwiches into egg mixture until well soaked. Sprinkle both sides with sesame seeds. Heat remaining butter and oil in a medium-size skillet. Fry sandwiches 5 to 6 minutes or until golden, turning occasionally. Cut each sandwich in 3 fingers. Garnish with unpeeled shrimp, cilantro and green onion slivers. Serve hot. Makes 2 sandwiches.

Welsh Rarebit

2 tablespoons butter
1-1/4 cups grated Cheddar cheese
1 teaspoon milk
1/4 teaspoon dry mustard
Few drops Worcestershire sauce
1/8 teaspoon cayenne pepper
Salt to taste
2 crusty slices whole-wheat bread
Tomato wedges and sprigs of fresh
    watercress to garnish

Melt 1 tablespoon of butter in a small saucepan. Remove from heat. Add cheese, milk, dry mustard, Worcestershire sauce and cayenne pepper. Season with salt. Mix well. Cook over low heat for a few moments until mixture begins to melt, stirring constantly. Remove from heat. Preheat broiler. Toast bread. Spread with remaining butter. Spread cheese mixture on buttered toast. Broil under preheated broiler 3 to 4 minutes or until golden and bubbling. Garnish with tomato wedges and watercress sprigs and serve hot. Makes 2 sandwiches.

Variation: To prepare *Bacon-Broccoli Rarebit*, cook 8 small fresh broccoli spears in a small amount of boiling salted water 5 minutes or until just tender. Drain well on paper towels. Cut off stalk so that broccoli spears fit on toast. Fry strips of bacon until crisp and golden. Place bacon over buttered toast. Top with broccoli spears and coat with cheese mixture. Broil until golden and bubbling.

Croque Monsieur

3 tablespoons butter, softened
2 (1/2-inch-thick) slices white bread,
   crusts removed
1 slice cooked ham
2 thin slices Gruyère cheese
Sprigs of fresh parsley to garnish

Lightly butter slices of bread on both sides. Cut ham and cheese slices to fit slices of bread. Place 1 slice of cheese and ham on 1 slice of buttered bread. Top with remaining slice of cheese and buttered bread. Press together firmly.

Cut diagonally in half. Heat a small skillet over low heat. Fry sandwich until cheese melts, pressing down occasionally during cooking. Turn once and cook until golden brown on both sides. Garnish with parsley. Serve hot. Makes 1 sandwich.

Variation: Substitute Cheddar cheese for Gruyère cheese. Spread cheese with pickle relish or ham with prepared mustard.

Giant Salad Burgers

1 lb. lean ground beef
3 tablespoons corn oil
Salt and pepper to taste
2 seeded rolls
2 green onions
3 tablespoons mayonnaise
2 tablespoons mango chutney
2 thick slices lettuce
2 slices large tomato
4 red bell pepper rings
Mild pickled chilies and tomatoes, to
    garnish

Form beef in 2 (4-inch) round patties. Heat oil in a medium-size skillet. Fry patties 5 to 6 minutes on each side or until cooked as desired. Season with salt and pepper. Cut rolls in half and lightly toast. Cut green onions in half. Using a sharp pointed knife, cut to form feath-ery ends. In a small bowl, mix mayonnaise and chutney. Spread bottom half of rolls with 1/2 of mayonnaise mixture. Arrange slices of lettuce on rolls. Top with slices of tomato. Place patties on tomato slices. Cover with green onions and bell pepper rings. Spoon remaining mayonnaise mixture over green onions and bell pepper rings. Cover with top half of rolls. To garnish, thread wooden picks with pickled chilies and tomatoes; push into each burger. Makes 2 burgers.

Variations: Omit mayonnaise mixture and top with ketchup or relish.

Add a slice of processed cheese or thin slices of Gruyère cheese.

Reuben Sandwich

2 tablespoons mayonnaise
Few drops hot-pepper sauce
1/2 small stalk celery, finely chopped
1 tablespoon finely chopped green bell
   pepper
2 thick slices cooked corned beef
2 slices Gruyère cheese
2 slices dark rye or pumpernickel bread
2 to 3 tablespoons sauerkraut
2 tablespoons butter
Celery leaves and green bell pepper
   rings to garnish

In a small bowl, mix mayonnaise, hot-pepper sauce and chopped celery and bell pepper. Place 1 slice of corned beef and 1 slice of cheese on 1 slice of bread. Spread sauerkraut on cheese. Spoon mayonnaise mixture over sauerkraut, then top with remaining slices of corned beef and cheese. Top with remaining slice of bread. Melt butter in a small skillet. Cook sandwich over medium heat 4 to 5 minutes or until heated through, turning once. Cut diagonally in half. Garnish with celery leaves and bell pepper rings. Serve warm. Makes 1 sandwich.

Variation: Substitute slices of pastrami for corned beef.

Vegetable Curry Pies

2 tablespoons corn oil
1 medium-size baking potato, grated
1 medium-size onion, chopped
1 medium-size carrot, grated
1 stalk celery, chopped
1 teaspoon cumin seeds
1 garlic clove, crushed
1-1/2 to 2 teaspoons curry powder
1 teaspoon fresh lemon juice
2 tablespoons frozen green peas
3 tablespoons frozen corn
1/4 cup chicken stock
Salt to taste
8 medium-thick slices white bread,
    crusts removed
1/3 cup butter, softened
1 tablespoon poppy seeds
Sprigs of fresh cilantro to garnish

Heat oil in a medium-size saucepan. Fry potato, onion, carrot and celery 3 minutes. Add cumin, garlic and curry powder; fry 2 minutes. Stir in lemon juice, peas, corn and chicken stock. Season with salt. Mix well. Cover and simmer 10 minutes. Meanwhile, preheat oven to 375F (190C). Using a rolling pin, firmly flatten slices of bread. Butter 4 slices on 1 side and remaining 4 on both sides. Press slices of bread buttered on both sides into 4 (4-inch) round pans. Trim edges. Fill with vegetable mixture. Using a 1-1/2-inch round fluted cutter, cut 9 rounds from each slice of bread buttered on 1 side. Place bread rounds, buttered sides up, in an overlapping border around edge of vegetable mixture. Press down lightly. Sprinkle poppy seeds around each bread round. Bake in preheated oven 15 to 20 minutes or until bread is golden brown. Garnish with cilantro. Serve hot. Makes 4 pies.

French Toast Fingers

1 egg
1 tablespoon milk
2 or 3 drops hot-pepper sauce
2 teaspoons tomato paste
1 small garlic clove, if desired, crushed
Salt and pepper to taste
2 slices whole-grain bread, crusts
    removed
2 tablespoons butter
1 slice processed Cheddar cheese
1 small tomato, thinly sliced
2 teaspoons chopped fresh chives

In a small bowl, beat egg, milk, hot-pepper sauce, tomato paste and garlic, if desired. Season with salt and pepper. Mix well. Soak bread in egg mixture. Melt butter in a medium-size skillet. Gently fry soaked bread until golden and crisp on both sides, turning several times. Remove from pan. While still hot, cover 1 slice of fried bread with cheese and tomato. Sprinkle with 1 teaspoon of chives. Top with remaining slice of fried bread. Press together lightly. Cut in 3 fingers. Garnish along center of fingers with remaining chives. Serve hot. Makes 1 sandwich.

Variation: To make *Sweet French Toast,* beat egg, milk, 1/4 teaspoon vanilla extract and finely grated peel of 1 small orange. Fry as directed. Sprinkle with a mixture of 1 tablespoon light brown sugar and 1/2 teaspoon ground cinnamon. Cut diagonally in quarters. Garnish with small orange twists and sliced fresh strawberries.

Chinese Salad Sticks

6 ozs. pork fillet, cut in thin strips
1 tablespoon sesame oil
2 garlic cloves, crushed
1 (1-inch) piece gingerroot, peeled, very
    finely chopped
2 tablespoons light soy sauce
Pepper to taste
2 tablespoons corn oil
4 green onions, cut diagonally in slices
1/2 red bell pepper, seeded, cut in thin
    slivers
12 small snow peas, ends and stems
    removed
1 French roll
1/4 cup butter, softened
Chicory leaves, torn in sprigs
2 ozs. fresh bean sprouts
Green onion flowers and additional
    slivers of red bell pepper to garnish

Put pork strips, 2 teaspoons of sesame oil, garlic, gingerroot and soy sauce into a medium-size bowl. Season with pepper. Mix well. Heat corn oil in a wok or medium-size skillet. Add pork mixture; stir-fry 4 to 5 minutes. Add green onions, bell pepper and snow peas; stir-fry 2 to 3 minutes. Remove from heat and keep warm. Cut roll in half lengthwise. If necessary, cut off a thin sliver of crust to make pieces of roll stand level. Spread with butter. Cover with chicory sprigs and bean sprouts. Top with hot pork mixture. Sprinkle with remaining sesame oil. Garnish with green onion flowers and additional bell pepper slivers. Serve at once. Makes 2 sandwiches.

Salami Cheese Melts

8 medium-thick slices white bread
4 slices salami, rinds removed
8 large thin slices Gouda cheese
1-1/2 tablespoons chili sauce
1 tablespoon chopped fresh basil
2 tablespoons butter, softened
Red bell pepper rings and sprigs of fresh
    basil to garnish

Using a 3-inch round cutter, cut 1 round from each slice of bread, salami and cheese. Spread 4 bread rounds with 1 tablespoon of chili sauce. Top with 1 round of cheese, 1 round of salami and another round of cheese. Spread with remaining chili sauce. Sprinkle with chopped basil. Top with remaining bread rounds. Press together firmly. Butter both sides of each sandwich. Heat a large skillet. Add sandwiches and fry over medium heat 2 to 3 minutes on each side or until golden and cheese begins to melt. Garnish with bell pepper and basil. Serve hot. Makes 4 sandwiches.

Denver Rolls

1/3 cup butter, softened
2 teaspoons prepared mustard
2 round rolls, cut in half
Chicory leaves
1 onion, cut in quarters, then thinly
   sliced
1 green bell pepper, cored, seeded,
   chopped
2 slices cooked ham, chopped
3 eggs
2 tablespoons cold water
1/8 teaspoon cayenne pepper
Salt to taste
Sprigs of fresh watercress and radish
   flowers to garnish

In a small bowl, mix 3 tablespoons of butter and mustard. Spread butter mixture on rolls. Cover with chicory leaves. Melt remaining butter in a small skillet. Add onion, bell pepper and ham. Fry over low heat until onion is soft. Preheat broiler. In a small bowl, beat eggs, cold water and cayenne pepper. Season with salt. Mix well. Pour egg mixture over ham mixture. Cook over low heat until light golden on underside. Place skillet under preheated broiler. Broil until omelette is just lightly set on surface. Cut in half. Fold each half and place between prepared rolls. Cut each roll diagonally in half. Garnish with watercress and radish flowers. Serve at once. Makes 2 rolls.

Salmon & Egg Croissants

2 croissants
3 eggs
3 tablespoons whipping cream
Pepper to taste
3 ozs. smoked salmon, chopped
1/2 cup grated Cheddar cheese
2 teaspoons chopped fresh parsley
1 tablespoon butter
Sprigs of fresh Italian parsley to garnish

Cut croissants 2/3 way through center, cutting from rounded side through to pointed sides; do not cut through crust. Warm croissants. Meanwhile, in a small bowl, beat eggs and cream. Season with pepper. Mix well. Stir in smoked salmon, cheese and chopped parsley. Melt butter in a medium-size nonstick skillet. Pour in egg mixture. Cook over a medium heat until just set and cooked through, stirring constantly. Open croissant and spoon in egg mixture. Garnish with parsley sprigs. Serve at once. Makes 2 croissants.

Saucisson en Brioche

1 (1/4-oz.) pkg. active dry yeast (about 1
 tablespoon)
2 teaspoons sugar
1/4 cup warm water (110F/45C)
2 cups bread flour
1/4 teaspoon salt
2 large eggs, beaten
1/4 cup butter, melted
1 (7- to 8-oz.) piece cooked beef sausage,
 about 2 inches wide and 7 inches long
1-1/2 tablespoons chopped fresh parsley
1 egg yolk, beaten
Sprigs of fresh parsley to garnish

Grease a large bowl. In a small bowl,
blend yeast, sugar and water. Let stand
until foamy. In a large bowl, combine
flour and salt. Add yeast liquid, eggs
and butter. Mix to a soft dough. Turn
out dough onto a lightly floured surface. Knead 5 minutes or until firm. Put
dough in greased bowl and cover with
oiled plastic wrap. Let stand in a warm

place until doubled in size, about 1
hour. Oil an 8-1/2" x 4-1/2" loaf pan.
Knead dough on a floured surface. Using a rolling pin, roll dough to a 9" x 7"
rectangle. Place sausage lengthwise on
longside of dough. Sprinkle sausage
with chopped parsley. Wrap sausage in
dough, overlapping dough on bottom.
Dampen edges and seal well. Put roll,
seam-side down, in pan. Pierce 3 holes
through to sausage along top of dough.
Put a roll of greased foil in each hole.
Cover with oiled plastic wrap. Let stand
in a warm place until dough reaches top
of pan, about 45 minutes. Meanwhile,
preheat oven to 375F (190C). Brush
top of loaf with egg yolk. Bake in preheated oven 30 to 35 minutes or until
golden. If necessary, cover with foil
during baking to prevent overbrown-
ing. Slice, garnish with parsley sprigs
and serve hot. Makes 6 to 8 pieces.

Ginger Banana Cream

2 tablespoons butter, softened
2 thick slices crusty white poppy seed
  bread
2 small bananas
1/3 cup whipping cream, stiffly whipped
1 teaspoon fresh lime juice
1 or 2 pieces stem ginger in syrup,
  drained
2 teaspoons stem ginger syrup
2 lime slices and sliced pistachio nuts to
  decorate

Butter bread. In a small bowl, mash 1 banana. Fold in 2/3 of whipping cream and 1/2 teaspoon of lime juice. Spread banana mixture over buttered bread. Slice remaining banana and dip into remaining lime juice. Arrange banana slices diagonally in overlapping rows on top of banana mixture. Cut stem ginger in half, then in thin wedge-shaped slices. Arrange between sliced bananas. Top with remaining whipping cream and drizzle with stem ginger syrup. Decorate with lime slices and nuts. Serve at once. Makes 2 sandwiches.

Peach Cream Croissants

2 croissants
2 tablespoons butter, softened
2 teaspoons fresh orange juice
2 teaspoons powdered sugar
2 ripe fresh peaches, peeled, pitted,
     thinly sliced
2/3 cup whipping cream
2 orange twists to decorate

Cut croissants at an angle 2/3 way through center, cutting from rounded side through to pointed side; do not cut through crust. In a small bowl, mix butter, 1 teaspoon of orange juice and 1 teaspoon of powdered sugar. Spread over cut sides of croissants. Arrange peaches in overlapping rows over bottom of each croissant. In a small bowl, whip cream until soft peaks form. Add remaining orange juice and powdered sugar. Whip until stiff and glossy. In a pastry bag fitted with a large star tube, pipe whipping cream mixture over peaches. Press croissant tops down lightly. Decorate with orange twists. Serve at once. Makes 2 croissants.

Variations: Substitute nectarines, strawberries, figs or kiwifruit for peaches.

Black Cherry Delights

1 (15-oz.) can pitted black cherries,
   drained, juice reserved
1 tablespoon cornstarch
1 tablespoon kirsch
3 tablespoons dairy sour cream
6 medium-thick slices white bread, crusts
   removed
2 eggs, beaten
2 teaspoons sugar
1/2 teaspoon allspice
1/4 cup butter
Additional dairy sour cream

To prepare cherry sauce, in a small
saucepan, blend reserved cherry juice,
cornstarch and kirsch. Bring to a boil,
stirring constantly. Reduce heat and
cook 2 minutes, stirring constantly. Remove from heat. Cut cherries in half.

Spread 3 tablespoons sour cream on 3
slices of bread. Cover with cherry
halves. Top with remaining slices of
bread. Press firmly. In a medium-sized
bowl, beat eggs, sugar and allspice. Dip
sandwiches on both sides and edges
into egg mixture. Heat butter in a large
skillet. Fry sandwiches 5 minutes or until golden brown, turning once. Meanwhile, reheat cherry sauce. Cut fried
sandwiches diagonally in quarters. Top
with cherry sauce and dollops of additional sour cream. Serve at once. Makes
3 sandwiches.

Variations: Substitute 1 tablespoon
orange juice for kirsch. Substitute
whole-wheat bread for white bread.

Peanut-Banana Sandwich

3 thin slices whole-wheat bread
2 tablespoon crunchy peanut butter
1 banana
1 tablespoon fresh lemon juice
1/4 to 1/2 teaspoon ground cinnamon
1 teaspoon soft light-brown sugar
2 ozs. cream cheese, softened
1/4 Red or Green Delicious apple, cored,
   to decorate

Spread 1 slice of bread with 1 table-spoon of peanut butter. Cut 2 slices from banana; dip into lemon juice. Reserve for decoration. Cut remaining banana in half crosswise, then in thin lengthwise slices. Dip into lemon juice. In a small bowl, mix cinnamon and brown sugar. Cover peanut butter with 1/2 of banana slices. Sprinkle with a small amount of brown sugar mixture. Spread 1 slice of bread with cream cheese. Place, cheese-side down, over sliced banana. Spread with remaining peanut butter and cover with remaining banana slices. Sprinkle with a small amount of brown sugar mixture. Spread remaining slice of bread with remaining cream cheese and place over banana slices. Press together firmly. Cut diagonally in half. Cut apple in 2 wedges. Dip into lemon juice. To decorate, thread reserved banana slices and apple wedges onto wooden picks. Sprinkle with remaining brown sugar mixture; push into each half. Makes 1 sandwich.

Chocolate & Orange Brioche

1 recipe brioche dough, page 83
3 ozs. semi-sweet chocolate, chopped
2 tablespoons ground almonds
Finely grated peel 1 orange
1 egg, beaten
Light-brown sugar, if desired

Let brioche dough rise, see method page 83. Generously grease a baking sheet. In a medium-size bowl, mix chocolate, ground almonds and orange peel. Knead risen dough on a lightly floured surface. Divide dough evenly in 12 pieces. Roll each piece to a 3-1/2-inch square. Place a small amount of chocolate mixture in center of each dough square. Fold long sides of dough over chocolate mixture and pinch seams together to seal. Pinch short side edges together firmly to enclose chocolate mixture. Roll each piece gently to form an oblong shape. Arrange rolls, joined-sides down, on greased baking sheet. Snip tops several times with points of scissors. Cover with oiled plastic film and let stand in a warm place until almost double in bulk. Preheat oven to 400F (200C). Brush rolls well with beaten egg. Sprinkle lightly with brown sugar, if desired. Bake in preheated oven 12 minutes or until golden brown and cooked through. Serve warm. Makes 12 rolls.

Variation: To create a differently shaped brioche, fit prepared rolls into well buttered tartlet pans.

Muesli Toppers

1/4 cup muesli
1 Red or Green Delicious apple, peeled,
   cored, grated
1/3 cup coarsely chopped mixed nuts
2 teaspoons fresh lemon juice
2 teaspoons honey
2 small oranges
2 thick slices raisin bread
2 tablespoons butter
1/4 cup cottage cheese, blended until
   smooth
8 fresh strawberries, hulled, sliced
Fresh whole strawberries and fresh
   sprigs of mint to garnish

In a small bowl, mix muesli, apple, nuts, lemon juice and honey. Using a sharp serrated knife, peel oranges and remove segments from skin membranes. Toast bread. Stand upright to cool. Butter toast. Top with cottage cheese. Cover with muesli mixture. Arrange rows of orange segments and sliced strawberries on top. Decorate with whole strawberries and mint. Serve immediately. Makes 2 sandwiches.

Variations: Substitute plain yogurt for cottage cheese. Substitute tropical style or other fruited muesli for muesli.

Sweety Pies

8 large medium-thick slices white bread,
   crusts removed
1/4 cup butter, melted
1/2 cup mincemeat
Finely grated peel 1 orange
1 egg, beaten
Julienne strips orange peel and whipped
   cream to decorate

Preheat oven to 375F (190C). Using a rolling pin, roll each slice of bread firmly to flatten. Brush both sides of flattened bread with butter. Press 4 sides of buttered bread into 4 (4-inch) fluted pans, pressing bread well into flutes. Using flat side of a knife, press firmly around edges of bread to cut. In a small bowl, mix mincemeat and orange peel. Fill each bread-lined pan with 2 tablespoons of mincemeat mixture; level surfaces. Using a small star-shaped cutter, cut a star from center of each remaining slice of buttered bread. Place slice of buttered bread over mincemeat. Using flat side of a knife, press firmly around edges of bread to cut. Lift edges of bread. Brush generously with beaten egg, then press edges firmly together to seal. Place pans on a baking sheet. Bake in preheated oven 20 to 25 minutes or until golden. Cool slightly. Meanwhile, bring a small saucepan of water to a boil. Add strips of orange peel. Cook 3 minutes. Drain, plunge into cold water and pat dry on paper towels. To decorate, in a pastry bag fitted with a plain tube, pipe whipped cream to one side of stars. Sprinkle with orange peel. Serve warm. Makes 4 pies.

Tropical Shortcake

2 (3-oz.) packages cream cheese, softened
Finely grated peel 1 small lemon
3 tablespoons whipping cream
1 shortcake, cut in half
2 kiwifruit, peeled, thinly sliced
Toasted blanched almonds and 2 mara-
**   schino cherries, cut in half,**
**   to decorate**

In a small bowl, mix cream cheese, lemon peel and whipping cream. Toast shortcake halves until light golden. Stand upright to cool. Spread each half with 2/3 of cream cheese mixture. Reserve 2 slices of kiwifruit. Overlap remaining slices of kiwifruit on top of cream cheese mixture. In a pastry bag fitted with a large star tube, pipe remaining cream cheese mixture in a rosette in center of each shortcake. Cut reserved slices of kiwifruit from 1 side through to center. Twist and place on top of cream cheese mixture. Decorate with almonds and maraschino cherry halves. Makes 2 shortcakes.

Asparagus Rolls

8 frozen asparagus spears
8 very thin slices whole-wheat bread,
  crusts removed
1/2 cup butter, softened
1/8 teaspoon cayenne pepper
2 teaspoons fresh lemon juice
2 tablespoons finely chopped fresh
  parsley
Small radish flowers and sprigs of fresh
  Italian parsley to garnish

Cook asparagus spears according to package directions. Drain well and pat dry on paper towels. Using a rolling pin, roll each slice of bread to flatten slightly. In a small bowl, mix butter, cayenne pepper, lemon juice and chopped parsley until soft and well combined. Spread 1/2 of butter mixture on flattened bread. Trim asparagus stalks to fit across width of buttered bread. Place an asparagus spear on 1 short end of each slice of bread. Roll up tightly, jelly-roll style. Wrap each roll in plastic wrap. Refrigerate 1 hour to chill. In a pastry bag fitted with a small star tube, pipe remaining butter mixture lengthwise along each roll. Garnish with radish flowers and parsley sprigs. Serve immediately. Makes 8 rolls.

Variation: Substitute canned asparagus spears for frozen asparagus spears. Drain well and pat dry before using.

Melon & Ham Fingers

2 slices pumpernickel bread, crusts
   removed
1/3 cup butter, softened
1 teaspoon fresh lemon juice
1-1/2 teaspoons tomato paste
1/4 small ripe honeydew melon, seeded
3 thin slices prosciutto, cut in half
   lengthwise
Sprigs of fresh dill to garnish

Cut each slice of bread in 3 (3" x 1 1/2")
fingers. In a small bowl, mix butter and
lemon juice. Spread a small amount on
bread fingers. Blend remaining butter
mixture with tomato paste. Mix well. In
a pastry bag fitted with a small plain
tube, pipe thin diagonal parallel lines of
butter mixture over buttered bread.
Refrigerate to chill. Using a small
melon baller, scoop 12 balls from
melon. Pat dry on paper towels. Thread
a melon ball onto a wooden pick.
Gather a half slice of ham and thread
onto wooden pick. Add another melon
ball to wooden pick. Arrange at a slight
angle over buttered bread. Garnish
with dill. Makes 6 pieces.

Taramasalata Stars

8 thin slices whole-wheat or white bread
3 tablespoons butter, softened
2 tablespoons toasted sesame seeds
6 to 8 ozs. tarama
4 pitted black olives, cut in slivers, and
**   sprigs of fresh parsley to garnish**

Toast bread until light golden. Stand upright to cool. Using a 2-inch star-shaped cutter, cut 8 stars from toast. Butter stars. Sprinkle sesame seeds over buttered stars; shake off excess. In a pastry bag fitted with a large star tube, pipe a generous rosette of tarama onto each star. Garnish with olives and parsley. Makes 8 pieces.

Variation: Substitute softened cream cheese for tarama. Substitute finely chopped chives for toasted sesame seeds.

Chicken Liver Sizzles

3 slices bacon
3 chicken livers, cut in half
3 large medium-thick slices white bread,
    crusts removed
2 tablespoons butter, softened
Dijon-style mustard
3 slices processed Cheddar cheese
Salt and pepper to taste
Corn oil
6 cherry tomatoes, cut in half, and sprigs
    of fresh watercress to garnish

Preheat oven to 375F (190C). Grease a baking sheet. Stretch slices of bacon on a cutting board until double in length. Cut each slice of bacon in half. Pat chicken liver halves dry on paper towels. Using a rolling pin, firmly roll slices of bread to flatten. Spread 1 side of flattened bread with butter, then mustard to taste. Top each slice of buttered bread with a slice of cheese. Cut each slice in half lengthwise. Add a chicken liver to each one. Season with salt and pepper. Roll up firmly, jelly-roll style. Wrap a bacon slice around each roll. Secure with 2 wooden picks. Cut each roll in half between wooden picks. Place on greased baking sheet. Brush lightly with oil. Bake in preheated oven 12 to 15 minutes or until cooked through and golden. Remove and discard wooden picks. Thread cherry tomato halves onto 12 wooden picks; push into each roll. Garnish with watercress. Serve hot. Makes 12 rolls.

Hot Shrimp Rolls

4 large medium-thick slices white bread, crusts removed
1 tablespoon butter, softened
2 tablespoons all-purpose flour
1/3 cup milk
2 teaspoons freshly grated Parmesan cheese
Finely grated peel 1/2 lemon
3 ozs. peeled cooked fresh or frozen shrimp, thawed if frozen, chopped
1 tablespoon chopped fresh parsley
Salt and pepper to taste
Vegetable oil for deep frying
1 egg, beaten
3 tablespoons dry bread crumbs
Lemon slices, peeled cooked shrimp and sprigs of fresh dill to garnish

Using a rolling pin, firmly roll slices of bread to flatten. To prepare sauce, melt butter in a small saucepan. Stir in flour and cook 1 minute, stirring constantly. Pour in milk. Bring to a boil, stirring constantly. Reduce heat and simmer 2 minutes, stirring constantly. Remove from heat. Stir in cheese, lemon peel, chopped shrimp and parsley. Season with salt and pepper. Mix well. Spread sauce on flattened bread. Roll up, jelly-roll style. Cut each roll in 5 slices. Half-fill a deep medium-size saucepan with oil. Heat to 375F (190C) or until a cube of day-old bread browns in 40 seconds. Meanwhile, dip each roll into beaten egg and coat in bread crumbs. Fry in hot oil until golden. Drain on paper towels. Thread lemon slices and shrimp on wooden picks; push into rolls. Garnish with dill. Serve hot. Makes 20 rolls.

Guacamole Pyramids

1 large slice white bread, crust removed
1 tablespoon butter
1 tablespoon corn oil
1 small garlic clove, cut in half
2 small ripe avocados
2 teaspoons fresh lemon juice
2 tablespoons finely chopped fresh
    parsley
8 peeled cooked fresh or frozen shrimp,
    thawed if frozen
Few drops hot-pepper sauce
Salt and pepper to taste
Small lemon twists to garnish

Cut bread slice in square quarters, then cut quarters diagonally in half. Heat butter and oil in a small skillet. Add garlic. Fry bread triangles until light golden on both sides. Drain on paper towels and cool. Cut avocado in half and remove pit. Using a small melon baller, scoop out 8 balls. Roll balls in 1 teaspoon of lemon juice and coat in parsley. Thread shrimp onto 8 wooden picks and add avocado balls. Scoop remaining flesh from avocado halves into a small bowl. Cut remaining avocado in half and remove pit. Scoop flesh into small bowl. Add remaining lemon juice and hot-pepper sauce. Season with salt and pepper. Mash well until smooth. Spread avocado mixture liberally onto fried bread triangles, making each a 3-sided pyramid shape by using flat side of a knife. Place wooden picks with shrimp and avocado balls on top. Garnish with lemon twists. Makes 8 pieces.

Celery-Pâté Sticks

4 ozs. soft smooth pâté
1/2 (8-oz.) package cream cheese,
softened
Few drops hot-pepper sauce
2 slices pumpernickel bread, crusts
removed
1 tablespoon butter, softened
2 stalks celery
2 radishes, sliced, and sprigs of fresh
parsley to garnish

In a medium-size bowl, mix pâté, cream cheese and hot-pepper sauce until soft and well combined. Cut each slice of bread in 4 (1-1/2-inch) squares. Spread lightly with butter. Cut celery in 8 (1-1/4-inch) lengths. In a pastry bag fitted with a small star tube, pipe pâté mixture in a diagonal design on buttered bread and down middle of celery. Arrange celery diagonally over decorated bread. Cut slices of radishes in quarters. Arrange 2 pieces on each side of celery and 3 pieces on pâté in celery. Add 2 small parsley sprigs to 2 opposite corners. Makes 8 pieces.

Variation: Substitute mini-toasts (crisp golden squares of toast sold in packets of about 33) for pumpernickel bread.

Mini Rye Clubs

4 slices pumpernickel bread
2 thin slices light rye bread
1/4 cup butter, softened
4 thin slices cooked beef tongue or ham
1/2 teaspoon Dijon-style mustard
2 small tomatoes, thinly sliced
Salt and pepper to taste
Fresh sprigs of watercress
2 ozs. Dolcelatte or other blue cheese
    cheese, softened
2 teaspoons mayonnaise
3 tablespoons finely chopped fresh
    chives
8 stuffed green olives to garnish

Using a 3-inch plain round cutter, cut 4 rounds from slices of pumpernickel bread and 2 rounds from slices of light rye bread. Butter pumpernickel bread rounds on 1 side and light rye bread rounds on both sides. Using same cutter, cut 4 rounds from slices of tongue. Spread 2 tongue rounds with mustard and sandwich together in pairs. Arrange slices of tomato over 2 pumpernickel bread rounds. Season with salt and pepper. Cover each with a pair of tongue rounds. Top with light rye bread rounds and cover with watercress. Spread cheese over buttered sides of remaining pumpernickel bread rounds. Place cheese-sides down over watercress. Press together firmly. Cut in quarters. Secure each piece with a wooden pick. Spread a straight edge of each piece with mayonnaise. Using a knife, press chopped chives onto mayonnaise to coat evenly. To garnish, thread olives on 8 wooden picks; push into each quarter. Makes 8 pieces.

Angels on Horseback

**6 shelled fresh oysters or 6 bottled or
  canned oysters, drained**
2 teaspoons lemon juice
**2 tablespoons finely chopped fresh
  parsley**
1 teaspoon Worcestershire sauce
Pepper to taste
2 slices bacon
2 large slices whole-wheat bread
2 tablespoons butter, softened
Lemon peel twists to garnish

In a medium-size bowl, combine oysters, lemon juice, 1/2 tablespoon of parsley and Worcestershire sauce. Season with pepper. Mix well. Cover and refrigerate 30 minutes. Meanwhile, preheat oven to 400F (200C). On a flat surface, flatten and stretch bacon slices to twice their original length using flat side of a knife. Cut each slice into 3 pieces. Drain oysters; discard marinade. Wrap each oyster in a piece of bacon. Secure bacon with wooden picks. Place oysters on a baking sheet. Bake in preheated oven 10 to 12 minutes or until crisp. Meanwhile toast bread. Using a 2-inch plain round cutter, cut 3 rounds from each slice of toast. Stand upright to cool. Spread tops and edges of toast rounds with butter. Coat edges in remaining parsley and sprinkle remainder on top. Cool oysters slightly, then place on toast rounds. Garnish with lemon peel twists. Makes 6 pieces.

Variation: To prepare *Devils on Horseback,* fill 6 pitted prunes with a small amount of mild mango pickle relish or hot pickle relish. Wrap each prune in a piece of bacon. Secure with wooden picks. Bake as directed above. Garnish with sprigs of curly endive.

Cheese-Cress Pinwheels

3 (1/4-inch) lengthwise slices uncut
   whole-wheat bread, crusts removed
3 tablespoons butter, softened
2 (3-oz.) packages cream cheese
2 teaspoons half and half
1 bunch watercress, stalks trimmed, then
   finely chopped
1 garlic clove, crushed
1-1/2 whole pimentoes, drained
Radish flowers and sprigs of fresh
   watercress to garnish

Using a rolling pin, firmly roll each slice of bread to flatten. Butter flattened bread. In a small bowl, mix cream cheese, half and half, watercress and garlic until soft and well combined.

Spread cream cheese mixture on buttered bread. Pat pimento dry on paper towels. Cut in thin strips. Arrange crosswise down length of bread. Roll up, jelly-roll style, starting from a short side. Wrap individually in plastic wrap. Refrigerate at least 2 hours. Remove plastic wrap. Cut each roll in 8 pinwheels. Arrange on a serving plate. Garnish with radish flowers and watercress. Makes 24 pinwheels.

Variations: Tint cream cheese mixture pink with a small amount of tomato paste. Substitute white bread for whole-wheat bread.

Salami Cone Canapés

8 ozs. soft smooth pâté
1/2 cup butter, softened
2 tablespoons whipping cream
1 garlic clove, crushed
Salt and pepper to taste
8 thin slices long loaf French bread
Chicory or red leaf lettuce leaves, torn in
   small sprigs
8 small thin slices salami, rinds removed
1/2 ripe avocado
1 teaspoon fresh lemon juice
Sprigs of fresh dill to garnish

In a small bowl, mix pâté, 1/4 cup of butter, whipping cream and garlic. Season with salt and pepper. Mix well until smooth and thoroughly combined. Spread slices of bread with remaining butter. Cover with chicory leaves. Press down firmly to stick to buttered bread. In a pastry bag fitted with a large star tube, pipe a border of pâté mixture around edge of each slice of bread leaving a slight hollow in center. Cut salami rounds from edge to center only. Form in cone-shapes. Place a salami cone in center of pâté border. Cut avocado in half and remove pit. Peel and dice. Sprinkle with lemon juice and spoon into salami cones. Garnish with dill. Makes 8 pieces.

Variation: Substitute cooked green asparagus tips or canned artichoke hearts, drained and cut in quarters, for diced avocado and lemon juice. Lightly toss asparagus or artichokes in French dressing and drain.

Glazed Chicken Canapés

1/3 cup butter
3 tablespoons all-purpose flour
1-1/4 cups milk
Salt and white pepper to taste
2 (1/4-oz.) envelopes unflavored gelatin
1-1/4 cups boiling chicken stock
4 to 6 (1/4-inch-thick) slices cooked
     chicken breast
1 whole canned pimento, drained
Cucumber skin
Sprigs of fresh parsley
8 slices pumpernickel bread
1/2 cup chopped pistachio nuts
Sprigs of fresh chervil to garnish

To prepare sauce, melt 2 tablespoons of butter in a medium-size saucepan. Stir in flour; cook 1 minute, stirring constantly. Add milk and bring to a boil. Simmer 2 minutes, stirring constantly. Season with salt and pepper. Mix well. Prepare gelatin according to directions, using chicken stock for liq-uid. Stir 1/2 of gelatin into warm sauce. Stir well, then pour through a sieve into a medium-size bowl. Using a 1-1/2-inch plain cutter, cut slices of chicken in 15 to 20 rounds. Place chicken rounds on a wire rack set over a plate. Coat with sauce, allowing excess to run off. Let stand 15 minutes. To decorate, pat pimento dry on a paper towel. Using an aspic cutter, cut pimento in flowers. Cut cucumber skin in leaf shapes and parsley stalks in stems. Dip decorations into gelatin and arrange on top to form "flowers." Let stand 15 minutes or until set. Spoon gelatin over "flowers" to glaze. Let stand 30 minutes. Using 1-1/2-inch plain cutter, cut bread in 15 to 20 rounds. Spread tops and edges with remaining butter and dip edges into nuts. Place decorated chicken rounds on buttered bread rounds. Garnish with chervil. Makes 15 to 20 pieces.

Cream Cheese Bites

4 slices pumpernickel bread
2 teaspoons dairy sour cream or
    mayonnaise
3 tablespoons very finely chopped fresh
    parsley
4 (3-oz.) packages cream cheese
1/3 cup butter, softened
1 tablespoon tomato paste
1/8 teaspoon cayenne pepper
1 to 2 teaspoons concentrated curry paste
    or 1 to 2 teaspoons curry powder plus
    1 to 2 teaspoons mayonnaise
1 garlic clove, crushed
6 seedless black grapes, cut in half
6 seedless green grapes, cut in half
Small sprigs of fresh chervil to garnish

Using a 1-1/2-inch plain round cutter,
cut 6 rounds from each slice of bread.
Spread edges of bread rounds lightly
with sour cream and dip into parsley to
coat. In a medium-size bowl, mix cream
cheese and butter until soft and well
combined. Put 1/2 of cream cheese mixture into another bowl. In 1 bowl, mix
tomato paste and cayenne pepper into
cream cheese mixture. In other bowl,
mix curry paste and garlic into cream
cheese mixture. In a pastry bag fitted
with a large star tube, pipe tomato mixture in a swirl over 12 bread rounds.
Clean bag and pipe curry mixture onto
remaining bread rounds. Lightly press
6 curry rounds onto 6 tomato rounds,
curry side up, and 6 tomato rounds
onto 6 curry rounds, tomato side up.
Place black grapes on tomato mixture
and green grapes on curry mixture.
Garnish with chervil. Makes 12 pieces.

Variation: Substitute white or whole-
wheat toast rounds for pumpernickel
bread. Coat buttered edges with poppy
seeds. Garnish with walnut or pecan
halves.

Salmon Cocktails

4 ozs. fresh or frozen white crabmeat,
thawed if frozen, finely flaked
2 tablespoons mayonnaise
1 tablespoon chopped fresh chives
Few drops Worcestershire sauce
Salt and pepper to taste
2 slices pumpernickel bread, crusts
removed
3 tablespoons butter, softened
4 ozs. thinly sliced smoked salmon
Red leaf lettuce leaves
8 lemon twists and sprigs of fresh dill to
garnish

In a medium-size bowl, mix crabmeat, mayonnaise, chives and Worcestershire sauce. Season with salt and pepper. Mix well. Cut each slice of bread in 4 (2-1/2" x 1-1/2")rectangles. Butter bread. Fold or cut salmon in 8 (4" x 2") rectangles. Spoon 1 tablespoon of crab filling on 1 end of salmon and roll up. Cover buttered bread with lettuce leaves. Place a salmon roll on top. Garnish with lemon twists and dill. Makes 8 pieces

Variations: Substitute toasted light rye bread for pumpernickel bread. Cover buttered bread with watercress sprigs. Substitute coarsely chopped shrimp for crabmeat.

Savory Boats

4 (1-inch-thick) slices white bread, crusts removed
Vegetable oil for frying
3 hard-cooked eggs, peeled
1-1/2 to 2 tablespoons salad dresing
Salt and pepper to taste
1/2 bunch cress
2 slices processed Cheddar cheese, room temperature
8 thin slices cucumber
4 cherry tomatoes, cut in half
Finely shredded green lettuce

Cut slices of bread in half crosswise. Cut off ends diagonally to form boat-shapes. Heat oil in a large skillet. Fry bread until golden brown on both sides. Drain on paper towels and cool. In a small bowl, mash eggs finely and mix with salad dressing. Season with salt and pepper. Mix well. Pile mixture onto fried bread boats. Using a knife, smooth sides to same shape as boats. Remove green leaves from cress. Press cress leaves onto sides of egg mixture to coat evenly. To make sails, cut cheese diagonally in quarters. Thread cheese and cucumber slices onto 8 wooden picks. Secure cherry tomato halves to top of wooden picks; push into centers of boats. Arrange boats on a bed of lettuce. Makes 8 pieces.

Variation: Substitute chopped salted peanuts for cress. Substitute drained canned salmon for egg. Flake salmon finely and mix with half and half or vinegar. Season to taste with salt and pepper. Substitute whole-wheat bread for white bread.

Ribbon Sandwiches

**2 large slices white bread, crusts
 removed**
**1 large slice whole-wheat bread, crust
 removed**
1/4 cup butter, softened
1 oz. Boursin cheese
**Sprigs of fresh watercress, finely
 chopped**
1 teaspoon half and half
1 large tomato, thinly sliced
Salt and pepper to taste
1 teaspoon mayonnaise
1/4 bunch cress
3 tablespoons salmon or crab pâté
**Radish flowers and sprigs of fresh
 watercress to garnish**

Using a rolling pin, roll each slice of
bread lightly to flatten slightly. Butter
slices of white bread on 1 side and slices
of whole-wheat bread on both sides. In
a small bowl, mix cheese and chopped
watercress until soft and well combined. Spread cheese mixture on 1 slice
of buttered white bread. Top with slices
of tomato. Season with salt and pepper.
Cover with buttered whole-wheat slice
of bread. Spread with mayonnaise.
Sprinkle liberally with cress. Spread
remaining slice of buttered white bread
with salmon pâté. Place, pâté-side
down, over cress. Press together firmly.
Cut in half crosswise, then cut each half
in 6 thin fingers. Garnish with radish
roses and sprigs of watercress. Makes
12 pieces.

———— Stuffed French Bread ————

4 ozs. sliced garlic sausage, chopped
1/2 cup salted cashews, chopped
4 green onions, chopped
1 small green bell pepper, seeded,
   chopped
2 stalks celery, chopped
1 (8-oz.) package cream cheese with
   chives, softened
1 tablespoon plus 1 teaspoon tomato
   paste
1 garlic clove, crushed
Salt and pepper to taste
1 thin loaf French bread
Green onion flowers and small tomato
   roses to garnish

In a medium-size bowl, mix garlic sausage, cashews, chopped green onions, bell pepper, celery, cream cheese, tomato paste and garlic. Season with salt and pepper. Mix well. Cut bread in half crosswise, then cut off crusty ends. Using a sharp pointed knife, cut away soft bread from inside of each half, leaving shell intact. Using a teaspoon, fill centers of bread halves with cream cheese mixture, pushing in well from both ends to prevent any gaps in filling. Wrap each half individually in foil. Refrigerate 2 hours. Cut each half in 10 slices. Garnish with green onion flowers and tomato roses. Makes 20 pieces.

Ham & Cheese Boats

3 large slices white or whole-wheat
    bread, crusts removed
1-1/2 tablespoons olive oil
1 garlic clove, crushed
1/4 cup finely chopped cooked ham
1/2 cup shredded Cheddar cheese
1 tablespoon tomato paste
1 tablespoon mayonnaise
1 teaspoon chopped fresh marjoram
Salt and pepper to taste
1 (2-oz.) can anchovy fillets, drained
3 stuffed olives, sliced, and sprigs of
    fresh marjoram to garnish

Preheat oven to 375F (190C). Using a
rolling pin, firmly roll slices of bread to
flatten. In a 1-cup measure, mix oil and
garlic. Brush over both sides of each
slice of bread. Cut slices in half lengthwise. Line 6 (3-3/4" x 2") boat-shaped
pans. Press oiled bread into pans firmly
by pressing another pan on top of oiled
bread. Trim edges with scissors. Place
bread-lined pans on a baking sheet. In a
small bowl, mix ham, cheese, tomato
paste, mayonnaise and chopped marjoram. Season with salt and pepper.
Mix well. Spoon mixture into pans. Using flat side of a knife, flatten surfaces.
Cut anchovy fillets in half lengthwise
and then in half crosswise. Arrange 4
pieces on each ham mixture in a lattice
design. Bake in preheated oven 20 to
25 minutes or until golden and cooked
through. Cool in pans 5 minutes. Invert
and carefully remove boats. Garnish
center of each boat with stuffed olive
slices and a sprig of marjoram. Serve
warm. Makes 6 boats.

Traffic Lights

2 large slices whole-wheat bread, crusts
  removed
2 large slices white bread, crusts
  removed
1/4 cup butter, softened
2 teaspoons Thousand Island dressing
2 green lettuce leaves, finely shredded
2 hard-cooked eggs, peeled, sliced
5 slices tomato
Salt and pepper to taste
Green onion flowers to garnish

Butter bread. Spread whole-wheat
slices of buttered bread with Thousand
Island dressing. Reserve a small
amount of lettuce. Cover 1/3 of each
slice of whole-wheat bread with
remaining lettuce. Remove egg yolks
from whites. Reserve several slices of
egg yolk. Arrange yolk slices over center of lettuce. Place 2 slices of tomato
over remaining area of each slice of
bread. Season with salt and pepper.
Using a small 3/4-inch plain or fluted
round cutter, cut out 6 rounds from
each slice of buttered white bread. Reserve bread rounds for another use.
Place slices of buttered bread over
tomatoes. Press together firmly. Cut
each sandwich in half to form traffic
lights. Chop reserved lettuce, slices of
egg yolk and remaining slice of tomato.
Fill relevant holes in sandwich. Garnish
with green onion flowers. Makes 2
sandwiches.

Variation: Substitute shredded Cheddar cheese for hard-cooked egg.

Party Sandwich Cake

1 large loaf whole-wheat or white uncut
    sandwich bread, crusts removed
1/3 cup butter, softened
1 (8-oz.) and 2 (3-oz.) packages cream
    cheese, softened
1-1/2 tablespoons prepared coleslaw,
    finely chopped
1 green onion, finely chopped
1/4 bunch cress
1 (3-1/2-oz.) can salmon, drained
2 teaspoons mayonnaise
1 teaspoon tomato paste
Salt and pepper to taste
2 ozs. Cambozola cheese or other blue
    cheese, sliced
2 tablespoons chopped red bell pepper
1 tablespoon plus 1 teaspoon milk
3/4 cup toasted almonds, finely chopped
3 tablespoons black lumpfish caviar or
    chopped chives and sprigs of fresh
    mint to garnish

Cut bread lengthwise in 4 slices. Butter bottom and top slices on 1 side and remaining slices on both sides. In a medium-size bowl, blend 2 ounces of cream cheese, coleslaw and green onion. Spread on bottom slice of buttered bread. Sprinkle with cress. Top with a slice of bread buttered on both sides. In a small bowl, combine salmon, mayonnaise and tomato paste. Season with salt and pepper. Mix well. Spread on buttered bread. Cover with another slice of bread buttered on both sides. Place slices of cheese on buttered bread. Sprinkle with bell pepper. Cover with top slice of buttered bread. In a small bowl, beat remaining cream cheese and milk until soft. Spread over top and sides of cake. Reserve 2 tablespoons of almonds. Coat all 4 sides with remaining almonds. Mark top of cake in 1-inch diagonal rows. Fill alternate rows with reserved almonds and lumpfish caviar. Garnish with mint. Slice and cut in fingers. Makes 30 pieces.

Anchovy Mosaics

1/4 cup butter, softened
1-1/4 teaspoons fresh lemon juice
1/2 (2-oz.) can anchovy fillets, drained,
  very finely chopped
1 cocktail gherkin pickle, finely chopped
1 teaspoon capers, well drained, finely
  chopped
1/2 to 1 teaspoon finely chopped fresh
  marjoram
1/2 teaspoon Thousand Island dressing
2 large thin slices whole-wheat bread
2 large thin slices white bread
2 or 3 (1/4-inch-thick) slices avocado
1 canned whole pimento, well drained,
  patted dry
Sprigs of fresh marjoram to garnish

In a small bowl, mix 2 tablespoons of butter, 1/4 teaspoon of lemon juice, anchovies, pickle, capers, finely chopped marjoram and dressing until well combined. Spread mixture on whole-wheat bread. Using a 2-inch fluted round cutter, cut out 4 rounds from each slice of buttered white bread. Using a small 1-inch star-shaped cutter, cut out centers of white bread rounds and discard. Place buttered rounds of white bread, buttered-sides down, over whole-wheat bread rounds. Press together lightly. Dip avocado slices in remaining lemon juice. Using 1-inch star-shaped cutter, cut out 4 stars from avocado slices and pimento. Place avocado and pimento stars on white bread. Garnish with sprigs of marjoram. Makes 8 pieces.

Herbed Quail Eggs

6 quail eggs
3 large slices white or whole-wheat bread
1/3 cup butter, softened
1/2 teaspoon fresh lemon juice
1/8 teaspoon cayenne pepper
3 slices (1/8-inch-thick) Sage-Derby or
**   Cheddar cheese**
1 kiwifruit, peeled
Finely shredded fresh sage leaves to
**   garnish**

Put quail eggs into a small saucepan of boiling water. Simmer gently 4 minutes. Drain and cover at once with cold water. Shell eggs and place in a small bowl of cold water. Toast bread. Using a 2-inch fluted round cutter, cut out 6 rounds. Let cool standing upright. In a small bowl, mix butter, lemon juice and cayenne pepper. Spread a small amount of butter mixture on toast rounds. Using 2-inch fluted round cutter, cut out 3 rounds from cheese. Cut each cheese round in quarters. Arrange 2 quarters of cheese at opposite sides on toast rounds, pointed-ends inwards. Cut 3 (1/8-inch-thick) slices of kiwifruit. Cut in quarters. Arrange 2 quarters of kiwifruit between cheese on toast rounds. In a pastry bag fitted with a small star tube, pipe a rosette of remaining butter mixture in center. Place a quail egg on top. Sprinkle eggs with sage leaves. Makes 6 pieces.

Selection of Tea Sandwiches

Selection of Sweet Sandwiches

Selection of Open-Face Sandwiches

Selection of Hearty, Layered & Long Sandwiches

Selection of Party Sandwiches & Canapés

Party Sandwich Cake, page 111

INDEX